FEARS, PHOBIAS AND PANIC

A Self-Help Guide to Agoraphobia

Maureen Sheehan

BA(Hons) MSc(Clin Psych) PhD AFBPsS

David Fulton Publishers

London

David Fulton Publishers Ltd.
14 Chalton Drive, London N2 0QW
First published in Great Britain by
David Fulton Publishers 1988

British Library Cataloguing in Publication Data

Sheehan, Maureen J.
  Fears, phobias and panic.
  1. Man. Agoraphobia. Self-treatment
  I. Title
  616.85'225

  ISBN 1-85346-055-9

Typeset by Chapterhouse, The Cloisters, Formby
Printed in Great Britain by Biddles Ltd, Guildford

Contents

With grateful thanks to David and Pam Fulton who persuaded me to put my thoughts on paper, to my sister Angela who helped to put them in order and to Christine Watson for typing the manuscript so beautifully.

To Lionel Haward, Iraj Mottahedin, Sandra Canter, Ian Gray and Peter Mayo who were my first clinical teachers.

To the Ville Gabrielle where this book began.

INTRODUCTION

The Problem of Fear and Panic

This book is for people who experience the type of fear that prevents them from doing what most of us take for granted. It is for the person who is frightened to leave the house or go very far from the house, who cannot go into shops or pubs, wait in a queue, travel on a bus or train, go to a cinema or theatre, or have a meal in a restaurant. It is for those of you who feel panic-stricken if you are left alone in the house or if you have to enter a small enclosed space such as a lift or bus. From time to time some of you may have experienced the very unpleasant sensation that you were not real or that things around you were not real. Others may have experienced the terror of a panic attack.

The fear of going out is often referred to as agoraphobia and the fear of being in enclosed spaces as claustrophobia. These two conditions frequently co-exist and the word agoraphobia is sometimes used as an umbrella term to cover both. Agoraphobia is also commonly associated with depression and with high levels of general anxiety.

Do not worry too much about these labels. Although the word agoraphobia means literally 'fear of the market place', it is rare for agoraphobics genuinely to fear being in open spaces. They usually experience some other fear. They may fear being ill out of doors, being abandoned, something going wrong at home, being trapped in some situation that they cannot leave easily (in a queue, in the hairdresser's chair, in the middle of a row at the cinema) and as a consequence feel insecure because they cannot reach a familiar place or face. Unlike other phobias, such as a spider phobia, the fear is not of

1

the street, or shop, or bus itself. These simply trigger distressing fear reactions, panic attacks or feelings of insecurity. They are cues.

For many people, the reason they are unable to go out readily is that at some time they have experienced feelings of faintness, nausea, or weakness of the muscles while they were out. Others have had a frightening experience such as a bus braking suddenly and throwing them off balance. Others describe the onset of these symptoms as coming 'out of the blue'. One day they were going out quite happily, shopping, travelling by bus, using the launderette, the next day they found themselves in the High Street feeling like jelly and having to get home as quickly as their jelly-legs would allow. The next time they attempted to go back to the same place they began to fear 'getting these feelings'. They report having lost confidence in their ability to go about their everyday activities. Many of them fear losing control and making fools of themselves in public. They fear being laughed at or ridiculed. Worst of all they despair of ever regaining control of this aspect of their lives.

Some of you may have had a full-blown panic attack which occurred without warning, and subsequently may have developed a phobia of going out or of being in the same or a similar situation to the one in which you had this frightening experience. Those of you who have experienced panic attacks will know how terrifying they can be. Your heart beats rapidly, you feel unable to breathe properly, your stomach cramps or churns, your legs feel weak, and you sweat and tremble. The fears that may accompany and intensify these feelings are of fainting, losing control, having a heart attack, going mad, or dying. No two people have exactly the same cluster of symptoms, but some of these symptoms will be familiar to you.

Not everyone who finds it difficult to go out has panic attacks. It may be that the person who fears going out has developed a phobia of the outside world and all its possible dangers. This fear may have arisen as the result of a terrifying experience such as being mugged or from reading about such cases in the newspapers. Sometimes the fear of the outside world is a red herring and the real fear is of something going wrong at home. In many instances, the fear arises after the loss of a loved and trusted relative or friend on whom the person has relied for security and support.

I have met many people in my practice as a clinical psychologist who describe their fears, their symptoms and what it is doing to their lives. Beyond them I know that there are thousands more who have not had any professional help and who are alone with their difficulties. As yet we have no idea how many people's lives are blighted in this way. Often they do not consult their doctors and ask for help because they are experiencing new and frightening feelings which they cannot put into words. They may fear that they will be considered to be mentally ill.

Whatever your symptoms are, and in whatever situation they occur, by now you will have many questions about what is going on in your body and in your mind. I hope that this book will help you to understand and overcome your difficulties and set you firmly on the path towards recovery. Over the last twelve years I have worked with scores of people suffering from these conditions and seen them gain control over them. I am talking about both men and women. Much of the literature in this field is slanted towards women and this is not surprising as the number of women who have sought treatment in the past far exceeds the number of men. Yet, in recent years I have treated as many men with these conditions as women. It is not clear to me why this is the case. Are more men suddenly suffering from these fears or has it become easier for men in the last few years to seek treatment? Whatever the reason it is important that men feel that their needs are also being addressed.

My interest in self-help for phobics started when I was a trainee clinical psychologist. At the time I was working at a hospital in Sussex and the department had a very long waiting list of people wanting treatment of agoraphobia, claustrophobia, panic attacks and generalised anxiety states. My supervisor suggested that I might like to start treating patients as a group. I selected the first eight patients from the list and saw each of them individually for an assessment at the clinic. As we felt that meeting at the clinic would encourage a strictly 'illness' view of these problems, we decided to look around for another more natural venue. Finally we got permission from the local council to use a room in the Community Centre. I arranged to meet the group there on Thursday evenings. Our programme was as follows.

After our initial 'getting to know each other' meetings, we settled down into the following pattern. During the first part of the evening each person discussed his or her problems and also what he or she was able to do in terms of activities related to the phobia. We then had a 'swap' session in which people who could manage shopping in large supermarkets offered to help those who could not manage them. Those members who had no difficulty with small shops offered to help those who did have difficulty. Similarly, with regard to travelling on buses and trains, people very soon offered to meet others at bus stops or suggested that they call in for a cup of tea after their journey. The group members found this kind of support particularly helpful. They felt that knowing that a friendly face would be there to greet them made any activity less of an ordeal for them. At the end of the evening we learned to relax together using the technique outlined in Chapter 4.

We were fortunate in that we did not attract too many 'professional phobics'. These are people who have made being phobic a way of life and who would find their lives empty and meaningless without their phobia. It was clear that although the two professional phobics we did have were more than happy to talk about their distressing symptoms, they were not attending the group in order to overcome their problems. They were there to foster the idea that it was better to learn to live with your problems, and it is doubtful whether we did much to alter their fixed positions.

Our membership quickly increased to sixteen when local general practitioners began to hear about us. This was really too many but we decided that we could always split into two groups if necessary. I am sure that in my ignorance I made

many mistakes. As I acted mainly as the co-ordinator, however, it was the group members who came up with the ideas. It
was important to ensure that the group did not treat me as an
expert and become too dependent on 'expert' help as I was
going to be there for a few months only and I was eager to set
up a group that would continue after I had gone.

There were several spin-offs for the group from our
meetings. Many of the members were isolated housewives
with small children and suddenly they were not only receiving
help for their problems but also building a network of friend-
ship, support and encouragement. Partners of the people in
the group used to come to the centre to pick them up at the end
of the evening. Gradually, they came earlier and joined in the
relaxation sessions. Later on several of them asked to join the
group so that they would have an opportunity to understand
the problems and to learn what they should and should not do
to help their partners. I am convinced that the success of our
group was in no small part due to the interest shown by these
family members and friends.

When it was time for me to leave, Nancy, a woman who had
been agoraphobic for thirty years offered to take over my role
as co-ordinator of the group. She had been able to overcome
her problems sufficiently to take a job as a cashier in a local
store and was determined to help others in their struggle back
to normal living. I do not want to give the impression that
Nancy overcame her problems simply through attending the
group. She had been having treatment for at least two years
prior to joining the group and felt strongly that had she had the
benefit of support from other sufferers earlier in her life she
would not have had so many years of misery.

This experience with the group taught me the value of self-
help therapy combined with knowledgeable and practical help
from others. Even though you may not feel confident enough
initially to start a group, you can always join one. Sources of
information about these and similar groups can be found in
local papers, doctor's/hospital waiting rooms and libraries.

The chapters which follow are about helping you to understand what is going on and to provide ways of coping with and

overcoming your fears. With luck, you will have the help of
friends and relatives and/or practitioners of one kind or
another, such as psychologists, behaviour therapists and
doctors. Without such help, you may feel totally isolated and
unsupported. Do not be discouraged. There is some recent
evidence that self-help can be as effective as professional
therapy. What you need is an understanding of your problem
and guidance in learning basic coping strategies. You do not
have to put up with the discomfort, distress and terror that you
feel now. Progress towards complete recovery may be quite
gradual and there may be setbacks along the way, (individuals
vary considerably in the time that it takes to recover) but if you
want to be able to lead a normal life, with determination and
patience you will get there.

To give you a glimpse of the kind of problems that are
referred to under the often misleading headings of
agoraphobia, claustrophobia, panic attacks and anxiety
states, I have included some 'conversations' between patient
and therapist. You may find that some of the patients have
problems similar to your own. The conversations are at the
end of the book, but you may like to turn to them now, or simply
dip into them as you read through the book. From them you will
get a feel not only for the problems we are dealing with, but
also for how the therapist handles the patient and builds a
relationship. If you are attempting to 'treat' yourself, you must
remember to be as honest, understanding and patient with
yourself as the professional therapist is with her patients!

Before you start to treat yourself, you need to understand
your own symptoms. Chapter 1 describes the physical aspects
of anxiety and panic, and how a phobia develops. It will help
you to understand what is happening to your own body when
you panic. You will be agreeably surprised to learn that your
anxiety is physically harmless and you are in no danger at all.

Having understood your symptoms, you need to get rid of
them. The easiest way is to take tranquillisers. These will
often lower a person's anxiety sufficiently to overcome the
phobia, but they may also become a crutch without which the
sufferer is helpless. Nowadays, we use a much broader

approach called cognitive–behaviour therapy. (This approach does not rule out the use of tranquillisers, particularly at the beginning of treatment when the person may need a chemical crutch until they feel strong enough to manage on their own.) The word 'cognitive' is the shorthand for the thoughts, beliefs, mental pictures and feelings involved in these phobic and panic disorders.

In practice, of course, we would deal with both the behaviour and the cognitions at the same time. In setting out to describe cognitive–behaviour therapy to a large number of unknown readers with a variety of difficulties, it seems simpler to present the cognitive part and behavioural part of the approach separately.

Chapter 2 deals with the cognitive part of the therapy. It is concerned with helping you to get in touch with your thoughts and feelings with the aim of learning how to modify them so that they work with you rather than against you. It is about changing the habits of a lifetime!

Chapter 3 deals with behaviour. It sets out to teach you how to control your bodily reactions using relaxation and anxiety-management training. Two principal methods are described. The first is called systematic desensitisation and is a step-by-step programme that enables you to overcome your fears gradually. The second is called flooding and it is what the name suggests. Instead of a gradual exposure to the situations that you fear, you are encouraged to stay in the situation you most fear until your anxiety has come down to a normal level. If you are in a hurry, this may be the treatment of your choice, but I do not recommend carrying it out on a self-help basis. This is a technique which has to be used with care as it is potentially dangerous for certain people. It should only be carried out by a clinical psychologist or psychiatrist trained in this technique.

Chapter 4 is for relatives and friends – the most important people in any therapeutic programme. In our department we always try to include a relative or friend in the therapy. Even if they have little time to be involved, their understanding of the problems experienced by the patient may be crucial. Often, of course, they arrive feeling as confused and alarmed as the patient and thirsty for an explanation of what has gone wrong. They want advice about the right sort of help to give to the phobic person. It may be that in their desire to spare the patient any distress, relatives are over-helpful. They go shopping, walk the dog, take the children to school, turn down social invitations and generally remove the necessity for the phobic person to go into situations that they fear. These helpers need to learn how to judge when to assist and when to fade out their help so that the phobic person gradually does more and more on his or her own. Most important of all, family and friends need to learn how to balance love and reassurance with encouragement towards independence. The sufferer needs a sense of safety but not over-protection.

Finally, and particularly if you are setting off on the journey towards recovery alone and full of apprehension, remember that you will never regret taking this first step. My good wishes go with you for a happier and more satisfying future without fear, phobias and panics.

CHAPTER 1

Understanding What is Going On

What is happening to you

A patient recovering from a phobia and who had just joined an evening class said to me the following morning: 'I felt very hot and sweaty during the first part of the class and I didn't take in very much of what was being said. Then we had a break for a cup of coffee and during that time I thought about what had been going on and understood it. Just understanding what was happening to me helped me to cope with the second part of the class.'

The patient was able to cope because he knew what was happening to him. He was able to interpret the unnerving sensations he had experienced and, armed with his understanding, was able to combat his anxiety.

More often than not, unfamiliar bodily sensations and high arousal levels are misinterpreted, and this can make them worse. If you interpret correctly what is happening to you, you can begin to manage your fear, panic or phobia. This chapter describes many distressing symptoms that you may have experienced and have no wish to be reminded of, but please try to read it. It will help you to understand what causes the symptoms, and this in itself will reduce your anxiety. Once you understand them, you may no longer have to dread such experiences in future.

Fear

We have all experienced fear. It is the emotion of pain or uneasiness we feel when we are faced with a threatening situation or danger. At its extreme, it is a state of alarm or dread. All types of fear can cause bodily changes such as your heart beating faster. In general when we are frightened we are likely to react with one of the three F's – freezing (silently rooted to the spot), flight, or fight. The difference between extreme fear and panic attacks is in the situations that trigger them.

Phobia

A phobia is a specific kind of fear that can develop in various ways. The word comes from the Greek word *phobos* which means 'flight' and is used to describe an exaggerated and often disabling fear. The characteristics of a phobia are an intense desire to avoid the feared situation. Phobias are emotional/physiological reactions which have become deeply ingrained habits. High levels of anxiety are experienced by the phobic person if he or she is exposed to situations that are feared.

Panic attacks

At the beginning of the book I described how many people experience a panic attack whilst away from home, in a shop, pub, hairdresser's, bus or train. Usually these experiences take place when the person is alone and away from home but they can also occur at home and even in the presence of someone familiar.

Panic attacks can be terrifying and may lead sufferers to think themselves seriously ill, mad or on the point of dying. This is not surprising if you consider the symptoms. When you have a panic attack your body behaves as if it is responding to a really perilous situation.

In conditions of real danger, such as reacting to a car out of control or facing a violent attacker, the part of the body that is responsible for how you respond is the sympathetic nervous system (which is part of the autonomic nervous system). This system acts quite automatically and prepares the body to take defensive action such as steering your car out of the path of an oncoming car, frightening off an attacker or taking to your heels. The body is in a heightened state of arousal. Among other changes, your heart rate increases, extra blood is pumped to the muscles, pupils dilate and your breathing becomes shallow. This last change often leads to over-breathing (or hyperventilation), which itself is often the cause of strange and worrying symptoms.

If you are subject to panic attacks, your autonomic nervous system has become over-reactive and is being triggered by quite harmless, everyday situations such as travelling on a bus. The physical changes that occur are the same as in conditions of real danger.

As well as physical symptoms, you will also experience changes in your thinking. You may find that you are very confused, unable to recall important facts, unable to concentrate and have difficulty in reasoning. At the core of these panic attacks may be fears of physical disasters, mental disorder or social disgrace. The combination of physical symptoms and thinking difficulties may lead to fears such as:

'I am losing control'
'I am not able to cope'
'I am going to collapse'
'I am about to have a heart attack'
'I am going mad'
'I am about to die'

The thoughts may be accompanied by visual images of hospitals, operating theatres, men in white coats, ambulances and coffins. The frightening physical symptoms, terrifying thoughts and images increase the anxiety and lead to an increase in symptoms and so the cycle goes on.

The next time you contemplate going to the shops, travelling by bus or underground train, your thoughts turn to what happened the last time that you were in that situation. Worrying about what might happen even before you are in the feared situation will almost certainly increase your anxiety. You may attempt to go back to the same or a similar place whilst feeling highly anxious and so increase the probability that you will again begin to feel panicky. You may have a full-blown panic attack. Thereafter, just thinking about the feared situation will produce some of the symptoms you experienced in the actual situation. You may become quite overwhelmed with panic and decide that you cannot go out or enter a shop or pub. The longer you avoid these situations, the stronger the fear will become, and you will develop a phobia.

All these symptoms are particularly frightening if you do not know what is going on. Understanding what is happening to your body and in your mind will help to dispel your fears. Let us look at some of the symptoms of panic attack and in particular those that are produced by hyperventilation.

Symptoms of a panic attack

Hyperventilation

Hyperventilation means overbreathing. We breathe in oxygen and breathe out carbon dioxide. If we overbreathe, we breathe out much more carbon dioxide than usual. This leads to a reduction in carbon dioxide pressure and provokes a marked constriction of the cerebral blood vessels. The result is a feeling of wobbliness. Like a balloon that has begun to deflate, you no longer feel firm and bouncy. All manner of physiological changes result from over breathing and the body has to work hard to restore the balance in the various systems which have been affected. When overbreathing is habitual, you may suffer from chronic symptoms. Here are some of them.

Neurological:
Central: dizziness, disturbance of consciousness, disturbance of vision

Peripheral: tingling sensations in hands and/or feet (parathesiae)

Cardio-vascular:
Palpitations, abnormally rapid heart action (tachycardia)

Respiratory:
Shortness of breath, chest pain

Gastro-intestinal:
Pain in the region of the abdomen (epigastric pain)
Feeling that you cannot swallow because of a lump in the throat (globus hystericus)
Difficulty in swallowing (dysphagia)

Musculo-skeletal:
Tremors, muscle pains

Psychic:
Tension, anxiety, irritability, inability to concentrate

General:
Weakness, fatigue, disturbed sleep.

As you can see, the symptoms can be quite alarming. Anyone of these symptoms may have led you to believe that you were physically or mentally ill. If you are unaware that your breathing is faulty, what else are you to think? In Chapter 3, I will describe how to improve the quality of your breathing. Slow, relaxed breathing is a crucial element in your fight to reduce tension and anxiety. You cannot be relaxed if your breathing is rapid and shallow.

Poor breathing is not of course the whole story. Two other very distressing symptoms are commonly experienced – not feeling real and feeling that your surroundings are unreal.

Not feeling real

One of the most dreaded symptoms that patients report is the sudden feeling that they are not real. Often they assume that this must be the start of a serious mental illness. The medical term for this symptom is depersonalisation. It is an extremely unpleasant and frightening state to be in and is described by patients in various ways. Some people describe it as a feeling of actually being detached from their bodies almost as if they were watching themselves from a distance. Others talk of feeling as if they have no sensation in their bodies and feel as if they are dying or disappearing. One woman described an occasion when she was sitting in a taxi and felt that the lower part of her body had disappeared. She was not aware of feeling particularly anxious and had had no warning that this might happen.

Feeling that everything around you is unreal

The medical term for the feeling that everything around you is unreal is derealisation. Again, descriptions vary from person to person: objects in a room may appear to be distorted or the whole room may look as if it is a stage-set. Although these feelings are very upsetting and possibly frightening, they serve a purpose. They are a defence against being overwhelmed with anxiety. Like an overloaded electrical circuit, the fuse cuts out.

Both these states may last for minutes or hours but eventually they pass.

Panic disorder and post-traumatic stress disorder

If you live in America, you will have heard the term *panic disorder* and may well have had it applied to your own problems. In the United States the term is used to cover anxiety, agoraphobia and depression which are seen as complications of this primary disorder – the cause of which is regarded by some as physical, although it is often associated with problems in relationships, bereavements and other stressful so-called 'life events'. In Britain and Europe panic attacks are regarded as part of a general anxiety state. Regardless of the name it's given, you will know the nature of the problem from which you suffer!

After any trauma such as a bereavement, an accident or assault, a bomb scare or fire, wartime imprisonment or torture, people may suffer what is called *post-traumatic stress disorder*. Recurrent intrusive images of the event trouble them for perhaps years afterwards and they are unable to rid themselves of the fears that surrounded the event. Other sufferers avoid thinking about the disaster and shrink from any situation that will remind them of it. This type of avoidance behaviour can be treated with systematic desensitisation, which is explained in Chapter 4.

How fears and phobias develop

Individual differences

In order to understand how fears, phobias and panic attacks develop, it is useful to know how individuals differ in terms of nature (what they are born with) and nurture (what happens to them during their life).

Taking nature first, people are born with a variety of constitutional differences. There is evidence that individuals are also born with differences in the way in which the autonomic nervous system and the central nervous system react. These systems may influence the development of a disorder so it helps to know the difference between them.

Autonomic nervous system

The bodily reactions that accompany fear, such as an increase in heart rate, dry mouth, shallow breathing, etc., are governed by the autonomic nervous system. According to your particular constitution, these bodily reactions may differ in the following ways:

- the reactions may be triggered more easily;
- the extent of the reactions may be greater;
- the reactions may last longer.

These differences can be demonstrated quite easily by the startle response. If you were sitting with a group of people in a room and a pop-gun was fired outside the room, there would be a range of responses. Some people might jump out of their seats whereas others might only raise an eyebrow. If it was a real gun being fired and an actual threat was presented the reaction might be even more varied; one person might faint whereas another might feel only an increase in heartbeat. The time it would take for all the people in the room to return to their normal level of arousal might also vary considerably.

If you were to change the conditions and just have a telephone ringing unexpectedly in the room, you might find that in some individuals this would trigger a powerful startle reaction whereas others would be completely unperturbed.

Central nervous system

The central nervous system consists of the brain and spinal cord. They 'receive messages' from the senses and send out signals to our muscles and glands. We hear a telephone ring and rise to answer it. But, in certain circumstances, we might not. We might be too scared to lift the receiver. One frightening experience might produce a 'conditioned fear response'. Suppose one night you are alone and you answer a call from a 'heavy breather' who says he's coming to get you. The door is locked, you know the caller cannot 'get you'. None the less, you are terrified. In future, every time the telephone rings, you are too afraid to answer it – even when you know the caller is a friend. You may even be unable to bear the sight of a telephone. Another person might receive a great number of such calls before a phobia would develop. Another person would decide not to answer calls in the middle of the night, and forget the whole episode.

Your background and environment

Apart from such differences in people's natures, there are differences in how people are nurtured. Their upbringing, home environment and the quantity and type of stresses that they have experienced over the years will be different. People with highly reactive nervous systems and an average degree of stress are far more likely to develop fears, phobias and panic attacks than others blessed with very stable nervous systems who have lived all their lives in peaceful surroundings.

It is also true, however, that many phobias develop without prior frightening experiences. Many people have severe fears of snakes, aeroplanes, germs and heights, without appearing to have had any frightening experiences associated with them. We know that fear or phobic responses may also be learned through the imitation of others. Mothers who are themselves frightened of going out or travelling on buses may 'teach' their children to fear such situations. This is because a great deal of learning takes place through modelling.

Is there a physical basis to panic attacks?

There is a great deal of argument as to whether or not there is a physical component in a person's vulnerability to panic attacks. Some researchers have suggested that there is a link between panic attacks and the following:

- high levels of caffeine
- the use of illicit drugs
- hormonal changes after childbirth
- hormonal changes after hysterectomy
- alcoholism (particularly during periods of withdrawal from alcohol).

Whether or not there is a physical component to your panic attacks, you can still learn how to control them. What is important is that panic attacks can mimic many medical disorders. For example, the symptoms of panic may be very like those that accompany heart attacks. At the same time, there are physical disorders that mimic panic attacks. For example, the effects of low blood sugar or thyrotoxicosis may be very similar to the symptoms of a panic attack and, for this reason, it is important that you consult your doctor so that he or she can exclude any physical condition that may be giving rise to your symptoms.

The sources of anxiety

Anxiety states and phobias develop in a variety of ways. Just one very frightening event may leave you with a lasting fear of encountering that or a similar situation again. We all know of people who grow up with a terror of dogs because they were attacked by a dog as a small child. If they have to go out of their way to avoid dogs, they have developed a dog phobia. This is relatively easy to understand because we can all see the cause and effect.

Other anxiety states and phobias may be the result of a long chain of events which are not nearly so obvious. Here are some known causes, starting with the most obvious.

Frightening experiences

Away from home
You may have suffered an unpleasant or frightening experience, such as

- being mugged
- feeling ill in a public place
- fainting in a public place
- being jolted whilst standing on a bus or coming down the stairs of a bus
- travelling on an underground train which stops unexpectedly in a tunnel for a long period of time.
- being involved in a road traffic accident.

Arriving home

- a fire
- a burglary
- a death.

After any experience such as this you may have begun to associate being out of doors or in an enclosed space with anxiety. Or it may be that anxiety has become attached to any of the specific situations described. For example, it becomes difficult to go into a shop where you have either felt faint or actually fainted. Unfortunately, anxiety spreads and soon you find yourself unable to go into any shop. Many travellers on the London underground reported feelings of anxiety after a big fire at a main station, even though they had travelled daily without fear until it occurred.

If you have had the unpleasant experience of coming back home and finding that the house has been burgled or, worse still, someone has died or a fire has started, you may well be reluctant to go far from home.

Stress

You may develop a fear of going out or experience an 'out of the blue' panic attack or fear of being alone because you are under a lot of stress. Many people live with stress for a long time and don't recognise the condition. Here are some of the more obvious life events which may create a build-up of stress or insecurity. Perhaps you have been

- having sexual and marital problems
- nursing a sick or dying relative
- trying to deal with a difficult spouse or child
- coping with the distress and disruption caused by living with an alcoholic partner
- dealing with unemployment and the frustration of trying to find work
- living with a violent partner and attempting to keep the peace
- moving house, particularly if you feel you have made a bad choice
- changing jobs and having to adjust to a new environment
- recently promoted to a position of greater responsibility
- recovering from a physical illness or surgical operation.

Stress may lead to a cycle of anxiety, overbreathing, muscle tension, physical symptoms and avoidance.

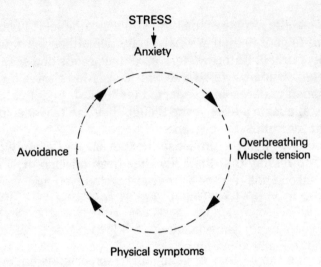

STRESS
↓
Anxiety

Avoidance

Overbreathing
Muscle tension

Physical symptoms

Low blood sugar and panic attacks

The medical term for low blood sugar is hypoglycaemia (not to be confused with hyperglycaemia, which is the condition where the person has too much blood sugar). The effects of low blood sugar are very similar to panic attacks. The symptoms include a feeling of weakness, sweating, increased heart rate, blurred vision, lightheadedness and tremors. Eating the wrong food and acute emotional stress may trigger hypoglycaemic attacks.

For example, consuming too many sugary snacks such as cakes, biscuits, sweets, chocolate, jam or drinks with a high sugar content will produce a sudden boost in blood glucose levels. This increase will give you an immediate spurt of energy which is quite short-lived and may leave you with *lower* levels of blood sugar.

A similar sequence of events may be the consequence of sudden emotional stress. During periods of stress the body's immediate response is to increase its output of adrenalin. Adrenalin is a hormone that raises blood glucose levels to enable our bodies to deal with an emergency. Consequently, after an emotional shock, our blood sugar levels peak. Often there is a rebound effect and blood sugar levels drop below normal limits. This is known as reactive hypoglycaemia. The symptoms are so alarming that they may trigger a panic attack. Subsequently, a similar situation to the one in which you experienced the hypoglycaemic attack may trigger a panic attack.

Latent anxiety

The fear reaction may be a response to an unrecognised source of anxiety. The apparent fear may represent a much less obvious fear. It seems improbable, but it is very often the case that the anxiety of taking on new responsibilities, such as a mortgage, a marriage or a baby, may lead to a fear of going out. Just thinking about new commitments may create anxiety.

Separation anxiety

A major component of agoraphobia is separation anxiety. A fear of something that might happen outside is often a red herring. It could be that the fear is to do with something happening at home such as a relationship going wrong.

Separation anxiety in adult life is very often the result of anxious attachment to a parent in childhood. Over many years the psychoanalyst Dr John Bowlby studied children who were anxiously attached to their mother (or whoever was taking care of them) and how this affected them later on in life. The fact that a child is anxiously attached to the parent may have been no fault of the parent. There may have been long periods when the parent was in hospital or there were separations for other reasons. Or the mother may have been depressed and unable to respond to her baby, and was therefore emotionally absent.

More dangerous for their child's future emotional well-being are parents who threaten to abandon their children as a way of controlling them. These types of threat are surprisingly common, and can be as extreme as threatening to commit suicide. Often children are made to feel responsible for 'driving a parent over the brink'. Dr Bowlby lays great emphasis on the terrifying consequences of threats to abandon children. Another source of later insecurity is the child overhearing his parents quarrelling and threatening each other.

Children who have grown up in stable families with a great deal of attention, encouragement and help are more likely to grow up to be self-reliant, co-operative, sociable and mentally healthy. Children who are anxiously attached are apprehensive about being left and terrified of being deserted. They are especially vulnerable to loss and depression. A great many disturbances in later life can be put down to disturbed patterns of attachment which endure throughout life.

Refusing school

Adults suffering from agoraphobia often reveal a childhood history of school refusal. School refusal can be linked to the anxious attachment of the mother to her child or vice versa. The commonest reasons for school refusal are that:

- the mother is herself extremely anxious and keeps her child at home to reduce her own anxiety

- the child fears that something dreadful will happen to their mother and so will try to stay at home to prevent it – for example, the parent may have made suicide threats

- the child wishes to stay at home to prevent the parent leaving.

Less common reasons are that:

- the child fears that something dreadful will happen to them if they go to school and so they stay at home to avoid danger

- The mother may have transmitted some of her own anxieties to the child

  the mother who is over-protective may fear that something dreadful will happen to the child when they are at school and so keeps the child at home.

Feeling unsafe

It is not difficult to see why adults who have felt insecure as children, because they have either been over-protected or lived in an unstable home, are vulnerable as adults. They are the people who strive to remain in familiar surroundings and at all times seek safety, particularly if they are under stress. Any loss – the loss of a husband, wife, relative or friend, either by death or because they have moved – may seriously affect our sense of safety. Other events such as an illness, during and after childbirth, a marital relationship going wrong, may also affect our sense of safety.

For the vulnerable person, any loss or major change will increase anxiety and they may find that they are unable to move from a place of safety or a safe person. Their anxiety increases if they feel that they are trapped in a shop, a queue, a bus, or if they have to meet a definite appointment. They may begin to restrict themselves to just a few familiar places and particular bus routes and to ensure that they are with a safe person wherever they go. They may be trapped in an unsatisfying, conflictual or even cruel relationship but fear having to live independently.

Fears of infidelity

Worries about infidelity seem to play a part in some phobic problems. A woman may worry about the possibility of her partner leaving her for someone else or vice versa. Either partner may insist that they are too fearful to be on their own. This may serve the purpose of keeping the partner bound to them.

On the other hand, there are men and women who fear that they might be unfaithful to their partners. In these cases, the phobia serves to keep them at home and away from the temptations of the outside world. Very often, the person is aware only of not being able to go out or to be alone. They are not aware of their fears about infidelity.

Bottled-up emotions

Perhaps you are a person who bottles things up? Instead of recognising situations which are full of conflict for you, you manage to tell yourself that all is well. Instead of feeling the sadness, anger, guilt, pain or resentment, you blank them out. Eventually all the pent-up feelings come out as symptoms of anxiety or panic. You don't scream, you have a panic attack. Your unconscious mind is aware of the problems and conflicts and of the feelings involved, but is unable to push through the barriers erected by your conscious mind. Anxiety states and panic attacks, although terrifying and painful, are a relatively safe way of releasing some of the feelings.

Thoughts and anxiety

Sudden changes in anxiety levels are often brought about by thoughts and images that intervene between an event and a feeling. These thoughts make you feel worse and maintain your uncomfortable bodily symptoms.

A ————————▶ B ————————▶ C

Event	**Thought/image**	**Symptoms of anxiety**
A delay in the queue at the supermarket check-out.	If I panic, I might scream or be sick.	Over breathing Heart pounding Dizziness

Beliefs and assumptions

Behind the thoughts that lead to symptoms of anxiety may be certain very firmly held beliefs and assumptions which make you vulnerable. They are usually of the black-and-white variety:

'I can't bear to be separated from others'
'I can't tolerate being out of control'
'I can't ask for help'
'I can't look after myself'.

Fear and depression

Any physical or behavioural problem tends to make you feel miserable. After months of struggling with crippling fears and of not being able to carry on your daily life easily and without anxiety, you become depressed. It is well known that anxiety and depression often go hand in hand and sometimes it is difficult to establish which came first and which is predominant. The same may be true of the more extreme forms of fear. Certain people develop phobias when they are depressed – some fear leaving the house; some making decisions; some driving; some being alone at home. These types of fears are said to be *secondary* to the depression. Once the depression lifts the person loses their fears. In such cases, it may be necessary to treat the depression rather than these secondary problems.

Breaching the dyke

By now you may be wondering where your fear, anxiety responses or panic attacks have come from. Many people have little insight into the source of their anxieties. Over months or years, anxiety and stress have been building up unbeknown to them. One day they experience symptoms of severe anxiety. Other people are able to point to a minor accident, illness or unpleasant event of some kind which appears to have triggered an anxiety state or phobia. In the latter case, by the time these individuals come for help they are quite convinced that the accident, illness or event was the starting point of their problems. They describe the disturbing event in great detail and are quite certain that their lives before this trauma were carefree. Before the event they appear to have been unaware of any conflict or stress and pin the 'blame' for their difficulties on the unpleasant event.

It may be that one traumatic event *is* the cause of the difficulties. After an accident outside the home, unless you can be persuaded to go out immediately, you may stay at home and in that way incubate your anxieties. For these cases, the cause is known and the treatment is relatively straightforward, although not necessarily quick or easy. Where the cause is not clear, it may take a great deal of detective work to unearth the difficulties, conflicts and anxieties that were there well before the starting point of the person's difficulties. What may then become clear is that the sudden shock of the precipitating event has been responsible for 'breaching the dyke'. Suddenly, and with enormous force, all the pent-up feelings, fears that have been hidden for many years, flood into consciousness and render the person helpless. The individual is literally flooded with anxiety and is unaware of how this anxiety has been gathering force.

Obviously there may have been many small streams and tributaries that contributed to the flood. Fortunately, we do not have to trace them all in order to learn how to manage the feelings.

CHAPTER 2

Getting in Touch with Your Feelings and Thoughts

Although we know that the body and mind affect each other, we often seem to forget that this is so. It is important to realise that changes in your thoughts and feelings affect your bodily reactions and vice versa. This is why an approach that deals with both is the most effective way of coping with these problems.

New psychological approaches

During recent years, new psychological approaches have been developed specifically for the treatment of anxiety. Of these, the one that has aroused most interest and research is cognitive–behaviour therapy. This type of therapy was pioneered by Professor Aaron Beck, a psychiatrist working in the USA who has been treating depressed and anxious people for over twenty years. Our two-pronged approach is based on his model.

At the end of the last chapter I talked about the various tributaries that may have fed your river of anxiety and panic. In clinical practice we begin to explore these tributaries from the start – attempting to understand the patient's feelings, thoughts, beliefs and mental pictures (their cognitions). At the same time we begin work on changing the phobic habits and faulty ways of thinking that create anxiety and panic. You, too, can use this two-pronged approach in your treatment of yourself, trying to change your behaviour and understand the

27

underlying causes at the same time. But, for the purposes of making clear how best to do both, I have treated each prong separately. In this chapter, I shall suggest how you can explore your cognitions. In the next, I'll concentrate on behaviour.

What lies behind anxiety and panic?

In many cases phobias and panic attacks are just surface manifestations of unresolved problems and conflicts. Our primary aim therefore is to solve these underlying problems. Sometimes this is not possible. Even if we are successful in following the problems to their source, the person often retains their phobic *habit* and conditioned fear reactions. These need to be treated with the methods outlined in chapter 3.

Feelings do not go away

Behind phobic fears and panic attacks there is often a phobic avoidance of expressing feelings – feelings of anger, resentment, need, love, affection or vulnerability. Many of you, because you have been struggling with unfamiliar and distressing feelings, have tended to try and keep all your emotions under strict control. Some of you, of course, have been doing this since birth because you have grown up in families where this is what was expected of you. Many people have grown up believing that any display of emotion is a sign of weakness. Your parents taught you, by their example, that certain feelings are either embarrassing or unacceptable. To express them is to risk the disapproval and rejection of others. You have been rewarded in subtle, or not so subtle, ways for being so controlled. Unfortunately, although you may be very skilful at masking them, feelings do not go away. Just because you are able to push your emotions out of sight does not mean that they lose their force. They just find another way of expressing themselves.

Whatever the feelings may be, we find that certain patients

who come with agoraphobic or claustrophobic problems, or who suffer panic attacks, lose these fears if they are helped to overcome the underlying fear of asserting themselves.

How safe do you feel?

Talking to patients it is clear that much of their phobic behaviour is designed to achieve and maintain a sense of safety. In general they do not feel anxious when they are with a familiar person or in a familiar place. One of the reasons for the widespread fear of sitting in the hairdresser's, queuing at the check-out, sitting in the middle of a row in the cinema, being driven in a car, seems to be a feeling of being trapped in a situation that you cannot leave easily. You cannot easily reach safety.

Behind this need to know that you can get to somewhere safe quickly is a general feeling of insecurity. How has this feeling of insecurity come about? One moment you feel perfectly safe going about your daily life and suddenly you feel about 4 years old. Often the change is the result of a threat to your safe routine or a sudden alteration in your life. For example:

- your husband/wife decides to leave you
- your son or daughter has announced that they are leaving home
- your husband/wife has just been made redundant
- a close friend or relative tells you that s/he is planning to move to another part of the country
- you discover that your partner is having an affair
- you notice cracks in the house you have just moved into
- you realise that you don't like living in the new neighbourhood
- you have been promoted
- your child has started school
- a close friend or relative has died
- you have to move because your partner's job has moved.

These are some of the more obvious changes in your life that can create enormous feelings of insecurity. It may be that you have not realised that there is a link between your fears, phobias, panics and the feelings of insecurity aroused by these changes in your life.

An understanding of why you are feeling the way you are and its links with the past will bring you closer to the source of your insecurity. Making links with the past may not be possible without the help of a therapist, but you can begin to make links in the present. Try doing some detective work.

Doing the detective work

When you feel anxious, tense and panicky for no obvious reason, your feelings are telling you that something is wrong. Emotional pain has the same function as physical pain. It is a signal that you must not ignore.

The feeling may not be related to the immediate situation. One patient, Peter, came for treatment because he had experienced a severe panic attack when he was travelling home from work on the underground. Subsequently, he was unable to travel by underground. Together we traced this fear to his unexpressed feelings of resentment and rage that he had said Yes when he meant No. One of his senior colleagues had asked him to work overtime and he had said Yes because he feared saying No. In talking about this incident, we discovered that throughout his life Peter had had difficulty in asserting himself. He had always said Yes to requests even when they were unreasonable or unfair. This pattern was repeated with friends, family and acquaintances.

As a consequence of this lifelong pattern of unas-sertiveness, Peter had built up a great deal of resentment. Rather like a kettle that has been steaming for too long, the lid gave way and some of the steam escaped. Unfortunately, as so often happens, the 'escape of steam' took place some time after the actual incident at work. It happened when he was travelling home on the underground. At first it was difficult for us to understand why he had had the panic attack. It was only after much talking together about what had happened during the day that we thought of the possible link between his inability to assert himself, his smouldering resentment and the panic attack on the underground. By the time he came for treatment he had developed a phobia not only of travelling on the underground but of shops and launderettes and cinemas. (You can read Peter's own account of his problem and treatment in the conversations in Chapter 5.)

You will need to do your own detective work if you suspect that there is a hidden feeling or unresolved conflict behind your fears and phobias. Sometimes the phobia, however distressing, may be preferable to looking at the conflict and trying to resolve it.

Can you name what you are feeling?

Think of the last time you were in a situation where you were feeling panic-stricken. Go through the situation in your mind or talk about it to a friend. Try to recapture the feelings you experienced then and during the 24 hours before the panic attack. Try to think about what was going on in your life and the circumstances surrounding this particular event.

Look carefully at anything that may have disturbed or upset you. At the time you may not have paid much attention to your feelings. Or, you may have put the wrong label on them. Many phobics label almost every state of high arousal as anxiety – feelings of anger, jealousy or frustration are commonly labelled as anxiety.

It is crucial, therefore, to recall accurately the feelings surrounding the onset of your fear, phobia or panic attack, particularly if it appeared to come 'out of the blue'. *It did not.* It came from you (even if there was a physical component to it). Try to remember if someone criticised you or made you feel foolish. Like Peter, you may have felt put upon or subjected to even greater injustice. You may have felt rejected, guilty, embarrassed or murderous. There may be a conflict in your life that you feel unable to resolve and which you have done your best to put out of your mind. If you find it helpful, write down exactly what you can remember of your feelings at the time. If you do this, you may be able to trace your way back not just to the emotions that sparked off your anxiety or panic attack but also to their actual cause.

A patient of mine, Graham, began to feel carefully into the circumstances surrounding his first panic attack and realised that there was more to it than the hangover he was sure had been the cause. The night before, he and his girlfriend, Lucy, had been out for a drink with a group of friends. After a few drinks, Lucy had started to flirt with one of his friends. Graham had ignored what she was doing and was not aware of the effect it had had on him. When he related the events that led up to his panic attack, he failed to remember until much later this crucial aspect of the evening out. This incident had had a powerful effect upon him because of its links with an earlier episode when he was on a field trip at school and his classmate girlfriend flirted with someone else. There may also have been events earlier in his life that had sensitised him to fears of rejection and abandonment.

Often people fail to associate significant life events with panic attacks. Another patient, Maggy, reported a major panic attack which had, as she put it, 'hit her' when she was out walking. She was so overwhelmed by the emotional and physical sensations that she had taken a taxi home. We spent several hours going over the circumstances surrounding this first attack which had set off her fear of going out. Finally, Maggy remembered that she had not just gone out for a walk. She had called in at the tax office to pay her bill. Not enough to trigger a major panic attack you may be thinking. However, the tax office was the one where her father had worked when he was alive. She had met one or two of the people who had known him and stopped to speak to them. As she remembered this, Maggy became very upset and told me that the last time she had visited the tax office her father had been alive and they had had a cup of coffee together. The panic attack was part of an unresolved grief reaction and there were a lot of issues regarding their relationship that needed to be talked about.

These examples of detective work were fairly straight-forward. Sometimes of course the feelings involved remain a mystery and we have to content ourselves with managing the anxiety so that the person can begin to lead a more satisfying life. If you find that you are not Sherlock Holmes, do not be too disheartened. Anxiety sometimes becomes so detached from its original source that it takes years and years to make the connections. You may not have time to do that if your life is disrupted by your fears. Fortunately, it is not always necessary to trace back all the links in the chain because some of the early links may be well and truly buried. Nevertheless, you can discover how your symptoms are being *maintained* in the present and you can learn how to manage your anxiety.

Listening to your feelings

Just as important as the detective work on recent and past events is learning to listen to your feelings in the present. You can do this by becoming more aware of your immediate reactions. Often your body, particularly your gut, will tell you what you feel but you may have grown used to ignoring this inner guide. Many of us try to hide our feelings even from our-selves.

Acknowledging your feelings

You do not necessarily have to act on your feelings. Just acknowledging what they are to yourself will relieve some of the tension. If you have grown used to ignoring your feelings you may find that there is a time-lapse before you register what it is you have been feeling. With practice you can narrow the gap and provide yourself with an invaluable source of information.

It is often said, and wisely, that you do not know what you think until you have said it aloud or written it down. The same is true of feelings, especially those that you would rather not feel – those that you push aside or ignore. A good way to

| **Mood Diary (1)** | | | |
Day and time:	Situation	Emotion	Remembered thoughts.
Monday 9 am	Waking up	Despair	Those palpitations again. I wonder how I'll get through the day
Tuesday 4pm	Collected my son from school	Felt low	None of the other parents bothered to speak to me
Wednesday 6pm	Colin (my husband) phoned to say he would be home late	Guilt	I'm such a nervous wreck, he can't bear to come home
Thursday 10am	Making beds	Anxiety	My marriage won't last if I say what I really think
Friday 11 am	Mother telephoned to ask if I had forgotten where she lived	Anger	She knows how busy I am

acknowledge your feelings (and a good way, incidentally, of relieving anxiety) is to write your feelings down. Make a diary of your moods. You don't have to show it to anyone else, so there is no need to be dishonest or embarrassed. Just keep a simple record of your changes of mood throughout the day. Set it out as in the example above, in an ordinary exercise pad. You'll be surprised how much you learn about yourself – and not only bad things!

Owning your feelings

The most basic step of all is to *own* your feelings. If you listen carefully to the people around you and to yourself, you will hear that all kinds of things are making them and you feel anxious and uncomfortable. Many people with phobias talk in a way that suggests that it is other people or external objects that are somehow responsible for their feelings. They say:

'Cinemas make me feel trapped'
'Waiting at the check-out in the supermarket makes me feel anxious'
'Sitting in the hairdresser's makes me feel terribly tense'.

These are some of the statements that I hear daily and I am sure that you recognise some of these statements as your own.

I find it helpful, as a first step, to get the person to take responsibility for the feelings and to change these statements to:

'I make myself feel trapped when I sit in the cinema'
'I make myself feel anxious when I wait at the check-out in the supermarket.'
'I make myself terribly tense when I'm sitting in the hair-dresser's'.

Take this first step yourself and try to change what you say to yourself and to others in this way. You can then move on to the next step which is to ask yourself *how* you are making yourself feel trapped, anxious or terribly tense. By doing this simple exercise, you will begin to feel a little closer to being in control. You will find that you are no longer quite so certain that these feelings are coming from outside of you. You may then begin to realise that you have a choice as to whether or not you continue to have these feelings.

The patient I talked about earlier, Peter, had never been able to own his feelings and to express them. Once he had learned how to assert his feelings, his panic attacks disappeared. Becoming more assertive is difficult, but once you have taken the first step it becomes more and more easy.

Overcoming anxiety with assertiveness

Assertiveness is being able to express what you feel, good or bad, and being able to ask for what you need or want, or to turn down what you do not need or want. It is the healthy way of responding to others. Unassertiveness can lead to all sorts of misery. It may make you a doormat. To be a doormat you have to suppress all your natural feelings of anger and resentment; you have to please others in order to survive. Being passive, manipulative and aggressive are all ways of responding that stem from a basic fear or lack of self-esteem. In your campaign against anxiety, you will find that assertiveness is a very powerful weapon. Anxiety leads to the suppression of feelings and particularly those that you feel to be dangerous such as anger. If you are angry, you fear that you will be rejected or abandoned. As we have seen, many phobic responses and panic attacks are a way of expressing some of these feelings indirectly. The only person who is harmed by them is you, although close relatives and friends may also be affected.

One of our patients, Peggy, was a striking example of unassertiveness. In her relationship with her husband she was excessively passive and submissive. She had had an extremely authoritarian father and her husband was a similar type. He dominated her completely and was critical of her clothes, her cooking and her friends. In order to maintain his dominance, he deterred her from having a job outside the home. It was clear that her depression and her panic attacks were directly related to her lack of assertive behaviour.

Although Peggy realised that she was behaving like a doormat, she explained that she felt terribly anxious and guilty if she expressed her resentment about the way in which she was being treated. She needed to learn that expressing her resentment would inhibit her anxiety. If she repeatedly asserted herself, the symptoms of her anxiety would gradually fade away. In her case, the symptoms of anxiety were overbreathing, panic attacks and the start of a fear of going out: As we have seen, the problem with anxiety is that it has a tendency to accumulate and to spread to other situations.

Learning to be assertive

It is difficult for anyone to recall specific incidents and feelings from a mass of everyday occurrences. Instead of searching your memory, it makes sense, once again, to keep a diary. Make a note of incidents and events involving others that left you feeling frustrated, depressed and unsatisfied. These events may seem trivial to the outside observer but if they have a powerful effect on you they are very important and should be noted down. Just completing the diary helps to focus your attention on the true source of your feelings. In addition to the event, note down how you felt, how you reacted and how you felt afterwards. At the same time think about the whole sequence of events and try to assess your behaviour and its consequences.

	Assertiveness Diary
Day, date, time:	Tuesday, 2nd February, about 8 a.m.
Event:	After breakfast, my wife said: 'Isn't it about time you asked for a better salary. You've never managed to keep us properly. We live like paupers.'
Feelings:	Very hurt and annoyed.
Reaction:	I went off to work as usual. I didn't say anything in reply.
Feelings/sensations:	Very upset. Terrible headache all day and palpitations towards the end of the morning.
Your assessment:	I can see that I should have said something to her at the time even if it was just: 'I find your remarks very hurtful.'

These diary notes help the therapist and the patient to isolate the particular difficulties each person has and to discuss new ways of responding.

Often fear of being direct about feeling and needs amounts to a phobia and is treated very much as we would treat any other phobia. For years the woman I talked about earlier,

Peggy, had been seething with resentment and frustration about being dominated and exploited but she was far too phobic to say what she felt. Instead, she became depressed and suffered from panic attacks. It was only when she found that she was beginning to fear leaving the house that she decided it was time to seek help. We used a step-by-step approach to help her overcome her anxiety about saying how she felt.

A step-by-step approach

Peggy kept a diary for two or three weeks and this enabled us to build a picture of the areas of her life where she was being unassertive and those where she was able to assert herself. Although Peggy was a dedicated doormat at home, if she had to make a complaint about the way in which her child was being treated at school she was totally fearless. We have found that many people are extremely assertive in most areas of their life but fail, for example, to be assertive in their more intimate relationships.

If you keep a diary for a few weeks you will begin to recognise the situations that make you feel frustrated, resentful or inadequate. You will begin to recognise your self-defeating behaviour. Once you are aware of how you need to change, you can use the step-by-step approach to overcome your anxiety. Select the least difficult situations to tackle. It may be that you have been suffering the frustration of dealing with a partner who constantly arrives home late in the evening muttering excuses about having to work late. It may be just a matter of saying to your partner: 'I feel angry when you don't let me know when you will be home. Please telephone me to let me know if you are going to be late.' If you haven't asserted yourself in this way for a long time, you may need to rehearse what you are going to say.

Your voice is giving you away

How you say something is almost as important as what you

say. In our clinic, we do not just rehearse what the person is going to say but the way in which to say it. We are careful to ensure that the responses we rehearse are not sarcastic, hostile or aggressive and that they take into account the other person's feelings and point of view. All too often, however, an assertive remark can sound quite aggressive if the person has an edge to his voice or his teeth are clenched. Using a video recorder, we demonstrate the difference between an assertive delivery and an aggressive delivery. The person is able to listen to the tone of his voice, and watch his body posture and his gestures. Even without the facilities of video recording, you can do a great deal to improve your delivery using a tape recorder and a friend to give you some feedback. With their help, you can learn if your voice is too soft, too loud or too scratchy. You may discover that you sound whiney, apologetic or that you are mumbling incoherently. Remember that anxiety restricts your breathing and this in turn affects the quality of your voice. Try to relax and deepen your breathing.

Your body is giving you away

Even if you say nothing, your body will express what you are feeling. In the case of the passive, unassertive person there are always body language give-aways such as hunched shoulders and hands which clasp and unclasp or fiddle with a handkerchief. These ways of behaving have to be *unlearned*. You need to become aware of the way you are using your body and your voice to convey messages about how you are feeling. Just by changing your body language you will begin to change the way that you feel. If you *act* assertively, then in time you will feel more assertive.

Many people when they are practising saying what they feel for the first time *look* extremely anxious. They give a very clear message that they believe that what they have to say is going to create unpleasantness. They have a 'don't hit me' look on their face or they smile placatingly.

Getting in touch with your thoughts

By now you are aware of how your bodily reactions affect you and cause alarm and terror. You are probably far less aware of the effect that your thoughts have on your feelings and bodily sensations.

Even if you have traced your problems to their source you may be left with the problem of a conditioned fear response and a way of thinking that helps to *maintain* your fears and phobias. Your thoughts influence your life in the way that advertisements influence what you buy. Some thoughts are not put into words. They are more like pictures in the mind or images. One of the most important messages for you to absorb is that thoughts and images produce feelings and sensations.

Fear of the fear

Many of you will know that just a thought or an image of going out, doing the shopping, getting on a bus, drinking in a pub, will produce some of the physical and emotional symptoms of panic. What you need to realise is that your fear is kept going by your alarming thoughts and images. Without the thoughts and images the panicky feelings would fade away very quickly. In the case of the person who is phobic, the thoughts fan the coals of their fear until they are white hot. Those of you who have experienced a sudden panic attack with no warning may develop a fear reaction to the place or situation where it happened. This is known as a conditioned fear reaction. Your mind and body are now conditioned to react with fear each time that you approach the same situation whether in reality or in imagination.

Panic may be triggered just by being in a place or situation that is similar to the original one. Normally the fear would die away fairly quickly, but if you start to fear that the reaction itself will lead to something worse – a heart attack or mental illness – then you will develop a fear of the fear itself. What happens then is that you attempt to avoid all situations that remind you of the first one and gradually your life becomes more and more restricted.

Panic cues

Those of you who have experienced panic attacks will no doubt be highly sensitive to any cue, however small or however false, that you are about to have another one. You react with concern or fear to any sensations such as an increase in temperature or heart rate. In a recent experiment a patient with panic disorder had a panic attack when he was given a false heart rate feedback. This is not the sort of experiment that I approve of, but it was a very clear demonstration of how a panic attack may be triggered. Your heart rate appears to have increased and you think: 'This must be the start of a panic attack.' When the tension creates muscle spasm, particularly across the chest, many of you will think immediately: 'I am about to have a heart attack.' And this *thought* alone will trigger a panic attack.

Automatic thoughts and images

Sudden changes in your anxiety level are often brought about by thoughts and images that occur between an event and a feeling. There you are, you've done your shopping, your trolley is full. As usual there is a queue at the check-out. Suddenly sweat is running down your face, your heart is pounding, and your legs are about to give way. What has happened? Nothing outside you has changed at all. One moment you were all right, the next you were feeling desperate. Something did happen, but you were not aware of it; it happened in your mind's eye. In a flash you thought 'If I panic, I may scream and go beserk', and you saw yourself pushing other shoppers over, upsetting trolleys, people laughing and pointing. You were making such an exhibition of yourself that you would never to able to face the world again. In a split second, this mental picture sparked off a physical reaction. And you didn't 'know' that was what happened.

Thoughts and images such as these arise very suddenly. They are well rehearsed so they can happen in an instant. They are not consciously summoned up. They arrive unbidden, and having done their damage depart as swiftly as they came. That is the secret of their success. Everyone has these 'automatic' thoughts that have a powerful but unconscious influence in their lives. Some will be true thoughts, which give us accurate pictures of the world and save us from danger; others will be false, warning of non-existent dangers and disasters. Because of this they are referred to as negative automatic thoughts or NATS for short. You may be surprised at the number of NATS that buzz around in your head. Clouds of them. These NATS have: (a) contributed to your fears and phobias; (b) helped to *maintain* your fears and phobias.

How to set about changing negative automatic thoughts (NATS)

Listen to what you are saying to yourself

First, you need to become aware of what you say to yourself. I know that this is easier said than done but you can become very skilled. Start off by monitoring your thoughts. Try to listen to what you say to yourself, particularly at those times when you become highly anxious. No doubt you will find that you are having 'panicky' thoughts:

'I must get out of here'
'I'm about to have a panic attack'
'This pain in my chest must be the start of a heart attack'
'I'm sure that blurred vision means that I'm developing multiple sclerosis'
'My hands are trembling; I'm spilling my drink. Everyone must be looking at me'
'What will happen if I faint'.

If you think you are going to panic you almost certainly will panic.

Count the NATS

Of course when you are highly anxious, it may be quite impossible for you to register what you are saying to yourself. You can make a start when you are less anxious by just counting the NATS. There are various ways of doing this. You can tick a small card each time you notice one. You can use a knitting counter or a golf watch. One patient I talked about earlier, Peter, tried this one evening. I had given him a golf watch for this purpose. He strapped it around his wrist and started to click it each time he caught a NAT. After an hour, he was so embarrassed by the number of NATS that he had caught that he gave up counting. It had been a very useful exercise as Peter had no idea of the presence of these NATS and how they were undermining him.

NATS do not really resemble the insects they sound like. They don't bite and fly away. They operate more like woodworm, slowly eating their way through the structure of your personality. If you have ever held what looks like a heavy timber beam and found that it was as light as a feather you will understand just how destructive woodworm can be. The NATS are just as destructive. Like the woodworm, their destructive activity goes on unnoticed. You are not aware of your NATS. They are invisible to you.

When you are able to do so, keep a record of your NATS. Begin by trying to catch one or two of them. Keep a notebook, a diary or a ruled sheet of paper and write down your thoughts, however unimportant or silly you may think they are. Most people find that writing the thoughts down is helpful because they are less frightening than they expected. You may find that you are facing some of your fears for the first time and that this alone will help to reduce them.

Challenge the NATS

Do not just swat the NATS or chase them away. It is far better to challenge them. It is very difficult to argue with the thoughts when you are aroused so wait until you feel calm and able to think properly.

The way to challenge the NATS is to ask yourself questions, like this:

Automatic thought: 'My heart is beating fast. I must be about to have a heart attack.'

Questions: 'Am I right in thinking this? Could there be another explanation?'

Alternative thought: 'I am very anxious and that makes my heart beat faster but it will not harm my heart.'

You need to learn to ask yourself questions such as:

'Is there another way of looking at what is going on?'
'Is what I fear likely or unlikely to happen?'
'What is the worst thing that could happen?'

What if it does happen?

Often people who are highly anxious avoid thinking through their worst fears. They are unable to think about what would actually happen if they fainted in the supermarket, had a panic attack whilst teaching a class of children or were trapped in a lift. Try to think about what would be so awful if what you most fear were to happen. You may find that what you fear would be less disastrous than you had assumed.

Early warning signals

Try to catch your thoughts as early as possible before your anxiety has a chance to increase. However trivial the thought may be, it could start the process that leads to panic. It is much more difficult to confront the thoughts once you have reached the point where you are so highly aroused that your thinking becomes distorted.

Try to deal with negative thoughts as soon as you become aware of them. You will notice from some of the conversations with patients in Chapter 5 that arguing with the panicky thoughts helps to calm you down. Giving yourself an alternative explanation, even if you only half believe it, will relieve the tension.

Positive self-talk

Practise talking to yourself positively when you are not in a situation where you feel anxious. Instead of saying to yourself: 'Don't be anxious', think of something positive to say to yourself such as:

> 'When I arrive at the party I will feel calm and relaxed'
> 'I shall attend to my breathing'
> 'I can cope'

Then, if you find yourself panicking, you can bring these thoughts to mind more easily. They will be waiting in the wings of your mind. Remember to talk your way through the panic. Give yourself positive messages such as:

> 'There is plenty of air in this lift. If it breaks down, there is an emergency button I can press to summon help. I am in no danger'
> 'These panicky feelings do not mean that I am going mad. If I sit down and wait they will pass'
> 'I am sweating but that is because the heat is quite intense in here. I shall ask if I can open a window or door'
> 'My heart is pounding and I feel clammy but there is nothing seriously wrong with me. If I breathe slowly and deeply and think of the word RELAX I shall soon feel calm, confident and relaxed'.

Positive automatic thoughts (PATS)

By now I hope that you are beginning to chase the NATS away with some really sound arguments or strong language. Do not be gentle with them as they are the saboteurs who will undermine any progress you make. They are the unseen enemy within.

You will need to replace the NATS with thoughts that will encourage your practice and help you to feel good about yourself and your efforts. Phobics are notoriously bad at giving themselves a pat on the back. You must begin to substitute positive thoughts for the NATS. As you begin therapy programme, start to praise yourself as lavishly as you can. Here are a few examples in case you have lost the habit completely and need help in thinking of what you might praise:

'That's very good, I have just reached my first target'
'I've done very well today. I carried out my relaxation and I practised going to the corner shop twice'
'I am really courageous starting this new step alone'
'I feel so proud of myself, I stayed in that shop until my anxiety went down'
'This week has been a great success, I am going to treat myself to a new pair of shoes'
'It is very sensible of me to stay at home today. I am far too anxious to go out. Tomorrow I shall feel much better and I'll carry on with my programme immediately after breakfast'
'What a marvellous person I am, in spite of my fear, I am travelling three stops on the underground'.

If you get into the habit of making positive self-statements these will become as automatic as the NATS. You will have substituted positive automatic thoughts for all those negative ones. Make your slogan: PATS instead of NATS.

Don't just 'half' believe what you're telling yourself, either. It is worthwhile trying to estimate how much you believe what you are telling yourself. Think of a scale from 0 to 100. At first you may be able to believe an alternative explanation only 50 per cent. Gradually you may come to believe it more and more. Add a note of how much you believe in your thoughts to your diary.

Distraction

If you have moved too far up the panic curve (see page 78) to talk to yourself sensibly, it may be possible only to try and distract yourself. Go for a walk. If you are in a place where you cannot do this, then count backwards from one hundred; count the number of people in front of you; look at the names of the streets you are passing, look for a particular colour, or think of something nice to go on your Christmas present list. Keep a postcard in your pocket with instructions on it to remind you what to do and then just wait for the anxiety to come down.

Beliefs and assumptions

Once you have got into the habit of collecting your automatic thoughts you will begin to recognise some of the ingrained 'beliefs and assumptions' that lie behind them. These are some of the extreme, all-or-nothing beliefs that clinicians have found to be common to may anxious patients:

> 'Saying 'No' directly is aggressive'
> 'I can't be left alone'
> 'I must never make a mistake'
> 'I can't allow others to be angry with me'
> 'I can't ask for help'
> 'To be in control, I have to be perfect'
> 'Failure is the end of the world'
> 'Unless I succeed, nobody will love me.'

Finding a response to irrational beliefs

No doubt you will find that you have a small number of beliefs or assumptions that keep your anxiety at a high level and that have never been challenged. Dig them out and begin to challenge them. Some of the beliefs may have started with the onset of your phobia. When anxiety is high it is extremely difficult to be reasonable or rational. It is important therefore to think about these irrational beliefs when you are feeling less anxious and to try to find more reasonable responses. For example:

Belief: 'I am not safe unless I am near to my home or to a hospital.'
Response: 'That is not true. I know how to look after myself and I can get help if I need to.'

At first you may not be able to believe in this reponse 100 per cent but at least you have begun to cast some doubt on your original belief. If you persevere, you may begin to believe it totally.

Cue card

When you have found an alternative response to your unreasonable belief, you may need to write the belief, and your response to it, on a card so that you can keep this in your pocket or handbag and look at it when you become anxious or panic-stricken. Or you might pin the card somewhere where you are likely to see it if you tend to become anxious when alone at home, or just before leaving the house.

The 'if only' syndrome

Sometimes the beliefs that maintain a phobia are more subtle than those I have talked about so far. To reach these beliefs you may need a more sophisticated approach. Dr Fay Fransella is a leading clinical psychologist who has used such an approach, called personal construct psychology, to look very closely at the way in which phobics think and what it is about their thinking that maintains the phobic state. She found that in some phobics there was a fantasy that life would be wonderful if only they were able to go out. They were reluctant to put this fantasy to the test and so remained phobic. Ask yourself if you have become trapped in the 'if only' syndrome. Do you sometimes say to yourself:

'If only I could go out, I would no longer have any cares or worries'
'If only I could go out, I would find myself a really interesting job'
'If only I could go out, I would leave my dreary husband and meet a really fascinating man'.

Whatever problem you are experiencing at the moment, if you dig hard enough you will no doubt find an unreasonable or irrational belief about it. It is these beliefs that give rise to the negative automatic thoughts. It may not be possible to reach them straightaway, but you can start the process of changing the thoughts that are closer to the surface of your mind and making them more realistic and positive.

Depression and your fears

I mentioned in Chapter 1 that depression and anxiety are often found together. It is not surprising if you are trying to cope with frightening and unusual symptoms that you should feel depressed about it. On the other hand, there are people who are depressed and as a *consequence* develop the type of fears I have been discussing. In their case, it is often necessary to treat the depression first. It is important if you feel that your phobia is part of a depressive illness that you consult your doctor as well as attempting to deal with the problem yourself. Depression is sometimes the side-effect of some physical condition and it is always wise to check on this. You may be interested to know what treatments are available for depression.

Current treatments for depression

Patients suffering from depression who consult their doctor may receive any one, or a combination of four forms of treatment. The first and the most widespread treatment is drug therapy using antidepressants and tranquillisers. For more serious depressions, electro-convulsive therapy may be used. For a small number of people, psychotherapy and cognitive therapy are offered. All these treatments have their place and have been found to be effective. They are not in competition with each other and can be used separately or in combination. Although the symptoms of depression have been found to respond favourably to antidepressants, some people are unable to take them because of a variety of medical conditions or because they cannot tolerate the side-effects. A large number of people who show improvements after a short course of antidepressant drugs relapse within a year or two of completing treatment. It seems to be important, therefore, for people who suffer from depression to look at some of the underlying causes as well as taking drugs.

Differences between depressive thinking and anxious thinking

When anxiety is the major problem, the person's thoughts are focused on *future* dangers and disasters. They are pre-occupied with how to avoid them. For the depressed person, the disaster has already happened. The depressive suffers from a feeling of loss, and particularly a loss of self-esteem. The loss may be of a person who has been very close or of some thing very important to the sufferer. The depressed person may feel that he has lost his confidence, his youth, his health or his hope of success. The future looks bleak and unchanging and, instead of avoiding danger, the depressive may endanger his life by neglecting himself or, worse still, by trying to kill himself. This depressive outlook may be the opposite of how the person viewed life before becoming depressed.

The person who is anxious without depression has not lost all hope, whereas the depressed person feels that he has nothing to look forward to except failure and unhappiness. He has a negative view of the past, the present and the future. The person who feels depression *and* anxiety usually fears he will never feel free of depression and free of the inertia that goes with depression. In a sense this type of anxiety when it accompanies depression is a sign that the person has not really given up hope.

Cognitive therapy for depression

As with the treatment of anxiety, you can use the cognitive

approach to help you overcome your depression. Ideally, I would recommend working with a therapist but this is not always possible as the waiting lists for treatment are long. Fortunately, there is a great deal that you can do for yourself.

Once again, your first step should be to see your general practitioner and to check on your physical health. You may wish to take antidepressant medication in order to raise your mood sufficiently to help you to help yourself. If you are feeling very low you may be so gloomy and hopeless that it is hard to believe that you have ever felt any different or that you will ever feel any better. Many people do not realise that they are depressed until someone close to them tells them that they are.

Take heart if you are feeling hopeless and helpless. Depression is the one condition that is self-limiting and you can certainly help to make it so. At the moment, perhaps, your depression is affecting everything you do. You may find that you have very little energy or enthusiasm for anything. What is the point, you think. You no longer feel interested in any of the activities that you used to enjoy. Worst of all you no longer feel warm and loving towards your family and friends. You certainly do not feel interested in sex. You are irritable and short-tempered. You may feel that you are unfit to be with other people and yet you cannot bear to be alone with your thoughts. This is where cognitive therapy can help.

Activity

Unlike the anxious person who may be restless and hyper-active, if you are depressed you may be almost inert and find it difficult to carry on with your normal activities. Some depressives sleep for much longer and find comfort in oblivion. Others wake early and lie awake tormented by hopeless thoughts but unable to rev themselves up for action. Others just begin to slow down and decrease their activities. They feel so miserable that they think: 'Oh, what's the point.' Or they feel confused and unable to make the mental effort involved in carrying out quite simple tasks.

Before looking at your negative thoughts and feelings, it is important to become more active because inactivity increases painful feelings and negative thoughts. Certainly, inactivity will not make you feel better, so it is worth trying to do more each day. I cannot promise that you will feel better immediately, but I can guarantee that your mood will begin to improve.

Once again try to keep a diary. Use the diary to list what you intend doing and then list exactly what you do do throughout the day. Depressed people, because they feel so negative, always underestimate what they do. The diary will be a more accurate historian.

Remember that none of us accomplishes everything we plan to do, so don't feel bad if you fall short of your expectations. The example below is a sample from the diary of one depressed patient, in which she records what she has done. Before she started her diary, Julie was convinced that she did nothing all day except sleep or loll about.

Activity Diary			
	Monday	**Tuesday**	**Wednesday**
7-9	Got up	Got up	Got up & dressed
9-10	Made tea	Made tea	Made breakfast
10-11	Went back to bed	Read newspaper	Washed up/made bed
11-12	Dozed	Made bed	Friend phoned
12- 1	Made toast	Made sandwich	Made sandwich
1- 2	Went back to bed	Dozed in chair	Read newspaper
2- 3	Slept	Did washing	Slept in chair
3- 4	Listened to radio	Sat down	Slept in chair
4- 5	Went to corner shop	Phoned mother	Took dog for walk
5- 6	Sat down	Peeled potatoes	Sat down
6- 7	Watched husband cook meal	Set table	Helped cook meal
7- 8	Ate meal	Ate meal	Ate meal
8- 9	Went to bed	Went to bed	Watched T.V.

Rehearsing

If you have been inactive for a long time, try to think of an activity or task that you feel you could tackle successfully. Go through each step in the sequence leading to the completion of the task or activity either in your imagination or verbally. Just by thinking about different aspects of an activity you may become aware of a negative thought such as: 'I won't be able to do it.' As you begin to change your behaviour, you can start to identify your unhelpful thoughts. You may find yourself thinking: 'At one time I could do all the housework and the cooking without giving them a thought;' 'I used to be able to hold down a high-level job and now I have to rehearse posting a letter.'

When you catch these NATS, remind yourself that in your present state you are carrying what feels like a heavy weight which affects everything you do. Certain physical symptoms are characteristic of depression and the most prominent are weariness and lack of interest. Everything you do may feel an effort and you may tire easily. You may also feel weighted down with your miseries. These feelings make it much more difficult for you to cope with normal everyday activities.

Faulty thinking

Having studied depressed people for many years Professor Beck, who was the originator of cognitive therapy, came to realise that the outstanding characteristic of the depression-prone person was his faulty thinking. It has long been recognised by clinicians that people suffering from depression have low self-esteem. Professor Beck noticed how negative the thoughts of the depressed person were, and perhaps more important that their thoughts were often distorted, not necessarily all the time, but at least during periods of depression.

What is clear is that your interpretation of what has happended to you will affect how you feel. If you misinterpret events in various ways so that the outcome, from your point of view, is always negative then your depressed feelings will increase.

What makes you feel depressed?

Patients often arrive saying that they have been feeling very low all week and they do not know why. If you are not used to paying attention to your thoughts and the feelings they produce, you tend to think that a change in mood has come from outside. Dare I suggest that you keep yet another diary. I promise it is almost the last!

The mood diary can be a notebook or a piece of paper divided into five columns. Note down any event associated with feeling upset or depressed. Then record how you felt and the thoughts that were going through your mind. Do this as soon as you can whilst the thoughts are still fresh in your mind. The fifth column is labelled 'alternative thoughts'. You can fill in this column when you are feeling better. Try to think of some alternative explanation for what has happened. As you are unlikely to believe completely in the alternative thoughts you come up with, it may be useful to assign a proportion of 100 per cent to each one to show the extent of your belief. You will then be able to see how you change in relation to these beliefs as the depression lifts. An example from a patient, Mary, I saw this week is given on the next page.

You may begin to see a pattern in the events you record and the way in which you interpret them. Mary is beginning to see that she is not always responsible for the behaviour of others. This is a pattern that, for example, many wives of alcoholics may recognise – these are the women who insist that their husbands drink too much because they are such dreadul wives.

	Mood Diary (2)
Day and time:	Monday, 8 a.m.
Situation:	My son Richard played me up when I was trying to get him off to school.
Feelings:	Irritation, then anger, then despair.
Thoughts:	He's really out of control. It's my fault. I can't stop myself nagging him. We don't seem to get on at all these days. I'm a terrible mother.
Alternative thoughts:	One tantrum doesn't mean I am a hopeless mother. 70%
	He has just started at a new school and is probably very anxious and on edge. 85%.

Other common errors in thinking

Thinking that you are personally responsible for someone else's mood is just one of a number of common errors in thinking in depression. Other very common errors which Professor Beck found were:

1. Taking one fact out of context and basing a conclusion on it. For example:
   'When I tell my wife what sort of day I have had, she doesn't listen. She obviously doesn't care for me any more.' (Ignoring the fact that his wife was attempting to serve a meal)
2. Making a sweeping statement about yourself after a single setback.
   'He didn't invite me out again, I must be totally unattractive.'
3. Making mountains out of molehills:
   'I couldn't follow what the teacher said today, I shall have to give up the course.'
4. Downgrading achievements:
   'Oh yes, I passed all my music exams but only because I worked so hard.'
5. Black or white thinking:
   'That sauce is all lumpy. I am a hopeless cook.'

It is obvious that the *meaning* that you give to an event will affect how you feel about it. If you *incorrectly* think that you

have been rejected you will react with the emotion appro-
priate to *actual* rejection.

As with the instructions for dealing with the NATS involved
in anxiety and phobic states, you need to challenge these
thoughts and develop different ways of looking at what happens to you.

Correcting faulty thinking

One way of counteracting a tendency to distort what happens
to you is to check your interpretation of events. You may find of
course that you are correct but that you have exaggerated or
distorted the significance of the setback. The woman who has
been rejected may feel that she is totally unlovable rather than
unloved by that particular person. The man who lost his job
may feel that he is a total failure and entirely worthless rather
than unsuited to that type of work. You need to discover for
yourself more constructive ways of interpreting the events in
your life.

Reality testing

Thoughts associated with depression often reflect the
person's feelings of incompetence, unattractiveness, social
isolation and general failure. These *ideas* are treated as *facts*.
They are not necessarily so. Try to examine the evidence for
your ideas. For example, Jane was convinced that no one in the
office where she worked liked her. No one had offered to help
her with the work or to take her to lunch. She was persuaded
to take the initiative and to ask a colleague to come to lunch
with her. To Jane's surprise her colleague was delighted to
have lunch with her. I can hear you saying to yourself that the
experiment might have turned out differently. The colleague
might have refused. If this had happened Jane might have
concluded that she really was unpopular. Our task would then
be to find out if this was true. We would reason that so far only
one person had turned down her invitation, and she would be
asked to invite another member of the department. If they all

turned her down we might want to investigate what it was about her that was being rejected. We would *not* assume that she was totally unlikeable.

Alternative explanations

Depressed patients are particularly prone to blame themselves for anything that goes wrong. We saw this in the case of Mary who felt that her son Richard's tantrum when getting ready to go to school was her fault. We had to go through all the relevant facts such as his starting to attend a new school, and not sleeping very well before she recognised that she was not responsible for his behaviour. Try to cultivate the habit of searching for an alternative explanation before pinning the blame on yourself.

Problem-solving

Depressed people, because of their negative bias, often claim that their problems are insoluble. They feel that they have tried everything and nothing has worked. They feel that they are and have always been incompetent and worthless. If you feel like this, try to go back over your life and find evidence of success and competence. Remember that most people when depressed are very clever at discounting whatever evidence they find that demonstrates that they have been successful in their lives. Once you have found and listed the evidence of your competence, you may begin to feel that it is worth looking for solutions to your current problems. For example, you may feel that you cannot manage your life without your husband, wife, mother, or child. Write down the things you think that you will not be able to manage alone. Look at your list and see if you have in fact managed situations like this on your own in the past. Then select the easiest situation to manage and try it out. This might be telephoning the bank to ask for an appointment to see the manager.

Underlying beliefs and assumptions

Distorted ways of thinking do not just arise because of some stress or loss in your life but relate to underlying beliefs and assumptions that have been with you since childhood. To protect yourself against further episodes of depression it is crucial that you begin to find out what these are. There is no quick, easy way of reaching these assumptions, though you can make a start by recalling important incidents from your past and discussing them with a friend or therapist. Family sayings can be particularly revealing.

Mark came to me after Christmas saying how depressed he was. At the office Christmas party there had been a present for each member of the staff – bottles of sherry for the men and boxes of soap for the women. There was no bottle for Mark. He said nothing at the time and assumed that this was the company's way of telling him that he was no good at his job. Mark 'took the hint' and composed a letter of resignation. I persuaded him not to send it but instead to ask his boss for an explanation. His boss was astonished. In the rush before Christmas he had delegated the job of ordering, wrapping and labelling the office Christmas presents to a temporary secretary, and had himself failed to check that everyone was included. He had a high regard for Mark and his work. Why on earth had Mark said nothing at the time?

This incident, which plunged Mark into depression, ruined his Christmas and nearly lost him his job, came about because of an assumption that he made without thinking, a belief that he had held since childhood without question. His parents always used to say, 'Don't trust anybody; the world is a dangerous place.' They stuck together and had few friends. They took offence easily. 'We can take a hint,' they would say at the slightest provocation. Mark had been 'taking the hint' ever since. He assumed insincerity on the part of everyone.

Together we examined how his parents gradually lost their friends and became estranged from their family because of their hypersensitivity and paranoia. Mark had been unaware how much his own reactions to people had been governed by these unquestioned assumptions. From now on he would try to make up his own mind about people and put more trust in them, starting with his boss.

Like Mark, you may be able to identify depressive themes that are associated with negative thoughts. Do you assume that you are a 'born loser'? Or, that the world is a dangerous place?

Seeking further help

When you have identified some of the underlying themes, you may well decide that you would like to investigate further. If you want to dig deeper to find buried causes and feelings from the past, it would be sensible for you to find a therapist or counsellor. You can analyse yourself only up to a point. Beyond that you may need a supportive and accepting relationship with a therapist over a long period of time. The security of such a relationship allows you to get in touch with feelings, emotional conflicts and experiences that have led to your present difficulties. Never be afraid to ask for help – remember you may be struggling by yourself because of an ingrained belief that 'you must stand on your own feet'!

CHAPTER 3

Changing Your Behaviour

Investigating the cause of your anxiety is important, but it often takes a long time, so it is wise to tackle your behaviour as soon as you have made an initial survey of your problems, and assessed the type and extent of the fears you suffer.

Changing our behaviour is always more easily said than done. Conquering your fears completely may be too difficult. So please don't expect a miracle cure. Remember that your aim is to learn how to manage your anxiety rather than to overcome it totally. It is perfectly normal and helpful to feel anxious at times, but it is not normal to be so anxious that you cannot get on with your life. Aim, therefore, to reduce the amount of anxiety that you feel and teach yourself how to manage it better. One of the first steps in anxiety management is to learn the art of relaxation.

Relaxation and anxiety management

There are not many certainties in the field of psychology but one fact that we are sure of is that you cannot be totally relaxed and feel anxious at the same time. Relaxing physically helps you to relax mentally. Learning to relax will help you not only to reduce your anxiety but also to do things more easily. That is one of the reasons why, in general, we advise patients to learn how to relax. (There are some exceptions to this general rule which I shall mention later.)

Many of you may have gone through your lives in a state of chronic muscular tension completely unaware of your condition. If you are in a state of high muscular tension you are a prime candidate for anxiety. Relaxation therapy reduces tension and is therefore a powerful antidote to anxiety. Just like any other skill, relaxation can be learned and programmed into the memory until it becomes second nature.

Breathing

I have described already the unpleasant and sometimes terrifying effects of incorrect breathing associated with tension. If you are able to achieve a state of deep relaxation you will find that your breathing becomes slower. This is because your body requires less oxygen and less carbon dioxide is produced. Paying attention to your breathing will not only help in your fight against tension but it will improve your general health. What you are aiming for is deeper, slower and more relaxed breathing.

If you are phobic, you will probably not have done much walking over the months or years that you have been troubled. Walking is one of the best respiratory stimulants. Many people become shallow breathers not just because they suffer from tension but because they are inactive. This is especially true of housebound phobics. What is more, the air that you have been breathing is not as rich in oxygen as the air outside. It is likely that not getting enough oxygen has added to feelings of confusion and tiredness. If you have taken very little exercise until now, do not rush into violent activity or you will just feel exhausted. Start gradually.

When you go out for a walk, this is the time to think about your breathing. Make a point of breathing more slowly, particularly if you are feeling under stress. Breathe out as much stale air as you can, pause for a second or two, and then breathe in the maximum amount of fresh air. As you breath out, think of the word RELAX.

Relaxation therapy

The exercises that follow (pages 66–70) are designed to help you to learn how to relax your entire body by alternately tensing and releasing muscles. Why create tension in your muscles when what you want to do is get rid of tension? There are two reasons. The first goal of this therapy is to enable you to recognise the difference between tension and relaxation of your muscles. This will help you to become more aware of muscular tension throughout the day. The second goal is to enable you to relax your muscles below their usual level. By tensing the muscles and then releasing them you create sufficient momentum to allow them to relax further. The principle is similar to that of a pendulum. If you want the pendulum to swing hard in one direction then the easiest way is to pull it back in the opposite direction.

One word of warning: some people become more anxious when they try to relax. This can be because they find it difficult to let go. Perhaps they have had to keep tight control over their feelings for so long that the idea of allowing themselves to relax is quite frightening. They feel that if they let go of their control, they will be out of control. Others find that the worrying or threatening thoughts that they have managed to keep at bay are able to slip past their defences when they are relaxed. If you are one of those who find that your anxiety increases when you attempt to relax, then try to find some other physical activity that you can do, preferably every day, that doesn't have this effect – going for a walk, jog, swim, dance or listening to your favourite music.

After your first practice session of the exercises that follow you may be concerned about how it went. Often people relaxing for the first time after years of tension experience sensations that worry them. Others want to assure themselves that they are practising correctly. These are some of the questions they ask:

Q. About halfway through the session, I begin to feel dizzy.
A. This is not uncommon and will disappear as you learn to relax.

Q. I had tingling sensations all down my legs.

A. Again, these sensations are quite common and are part of becoming relaxed.
Q. The next day my neck and shoulders felt quite stiff.
A. Remember to tense your muscles only enough to feel the difference between tension and relaxation.
Q. I noticed that my stomach (neck, jaw) was still tense when the rest of my body was relaxed.
A. Pay special attention to the areas of your body that become particularly tense. If necessary go through the tension/release cycle for the muscle groups in that area two or three times.
Q. Thoughts keep going through my mind when I am trying to relax. What should I do about them?
A. Just allow the thoughts to come into your mind and go out again. If you struggle to keep them out you will begin to feel tense. If the thoughts make you feel very uncomfortable, try to distract yourself by focusing on your breathing. Remember the mind is often the last part of you to become relaxed. Persevere with the practice and soon you will feel totally relaxed.
Q. I fell asleep whilst I was relaxing.
A. That is perfectly all right if you have the time. Some people prefer to carry out the relaxation exercises before going to bed and they enjoy a relaxed sleep. Many people sleep in a very tense way, as witness those individuals who grind their teeth or suffer from nightmares and night terrors.
    If you need to be awake immediately after your practice, set an alarm or cooking timer to wake you up.
Q. Does it matter if I do the exercises in a different order?
A. No, it does not, although it is best to stick to a certain order whilst you are learning as there is less likelihood then that you will leave out one of the muscle groups.

Relaxation aids

Make a tape
You cannot follow the book while you do the exercises and it

may be difficult to memorize them. An easy way round the problem is to follow a tape-recorded set of instructions. You can buy relaxation tapes or make your own. If you decide to make your own, read through the exercises once or twice and then tape-record your own voice giving instructions. You may have to do this more than once because the timing is very important. If you think someone else's voice would be more soothing, ask a friend to read the instructions. Once you get used to the procedure you may want to go through the exercises without the tape.

Music to relax to

Many people find that when they are used to the relaxation procedure, tape-recorded music helps them to relax more deeply. Find a piece of music that does not require too much of your attention but will serve as a background. Use the same piece of music each time you relax and it will act as a cue.

The relaxation habit

Before you begin your training it is a good idea to think about when and where in your daily routine you will be able to carry out your practice sessions. Try to do the relaxation at the same time every day so that it becomes a habit. Keep a chart with the times that you have decided on and tick each occasion that you complete your practice.

Carrying out the relaxation even when you feel reasonably calm is rather like putting money in the bank for a rainy day. You need to be able to draw on the relaxation response whenever you feel your anxiety level increasing.

Relaxation procedure

Choose a warm, fairly quiet room and ensure as far as possible that you will not be disturbed (e.g. take the telephone off the hook) and warn your family and friends not to disturb you for half an hour except for emergencies.

Make sure your clothing is comfortable by loosening ties,

belts, collars, etc., and removing your shoes. Reduce light and noise from outside by drawing curtains and closing windows where possible.

Lie flat on your back on a full-length sofa, bed or on the floor (if you use the floor make sure that you have a large towel or mat to lie on). If it is not possible to lie down, sit in a comfortable chair. In either case have your legs outstretched and uncrossed and your arms by your sides.

Before you begin the tension–relaxation exercises, close your eyes and let yourself become as comfortable as you can. Each tension–release cycle should begin with 6–8 seconds of tension and be followed by up to 1 minute of relaxation.

Ensure that you become aware of tension and relaxation; it is essential that you are able to tell the difference between these two states. This will help you to become more aware of your bodily feelings at other times.

Most important of all, pay attention to your breathing. You will notice after you have been tensing your muscles that your breathing has changed. When you relax, make sure that your breathing is regular and try to think of the word RELAX as you breathe out and your body relaxes.

Remember that relaxation is a skill which has to be learned and therefore requires practice if it is to be learned properly. Learning proceeds initially through many small steps which are then combined and reduced to the point where you can relax whenever you want to. Meanwhile, practise for at least 15–20 minutes a day, and twice a day if possible. This is an active treatment. It is not like a pill which is taken and then forgotten.

TENSION–RELAXATION EXERCISES

In the tension–relaxation sequences that follow remember to hold the tension for *6–8 seconds* and then relax the muscles for *30–40 seconds*. If the muscle group does not feel completely relaxed then repeat the sequence and this time relax the muscles for *45–60 seconds*.

If you have been in a state of chronic tension it may be

difficult for you to judge how relaxed the muscles are and
therefore it is a good idea to repeat the sequences.

1. *Forehead*

   Tension strategy
   With eyes closed, raise both eyebrows as high as possible
   and hold them in this position. (If you feel any eye-ache,
   release the tension.)

   Relaxation
   Now let your brows drop and relax. Smooth out your forehead and let all the muscles relax and unwind.
   Remember to breathe evenly and, as you breathe out,
   think of the word RELAX.

2. *Upper cheeks and nose*

   Tension strategy
   Screw up your eyes and wrinkle your nose and generally
   make a horrible face. (If you feel any eye-ache, release the
   tension immediately.)

   Relaxation
   Let go and relax your face and keep your eyelids lightly
   closed. Remember to breathe evenly, and as you breathe
   out, think of the word RELAX.

3. *Lower cheeks and jaws/neck (front)*

   Tension strategy
   Bite your teeth together, part your lips slightly and pull
   back the corners of your mouth.

   Relaxation
   Now relax your jaw. Let your jaw become loose and
   floppy. Remember to breathe evenly and, as you breathe
   out, think of the word RELAX.

4. *Shoulders and upper back*

Tension strategy
Shrug your shoulders. Bring your shoulders up towards your ears as high as you can and as hard as you can.

Relaxation
Let your shoulders drop down and relax, and feel the tension ease away. Allow the muscles to go on relaxing more and more.

5. (a) *Neck muscles*

Tension strategy
Press your head back as hard as you can into the bed or chair.

Relaxation
Bring your head back to its resting position on the bed or chair and RELAX.

(b) *Neck Muscles*

Tension strategy
Slowly raise your head and bring your chin down towards your chest and at the same time try to prevent it from actually touching the chest. Then slowly, slowly bring the head back on to the pillow or chair.

Relaxation
Let your head rest in its normal position on the bed or chair and RELAX.

6. *Chest*

Tension strategy
Tense the muscles of your chest by breathing in as deeply as you can. Breathe deeper and deeper and then hold your breath and feel the tension in your chest.

Relaxation
Breathe out and relax.

7. *Back and buttocks*

   Tension strategy
   Try and pull your shoulder blades together, and at the same time arch your back and tense your buttocks.

   Relaxation
   Relax back into your lying or sitting position.

8. *Hands, forearms and triceps*
   At first this strategy may be carried out with each arm separately.

   Tension strategy
   With your arms by your sides, make tight fists with your hands. Feel the tension in your knuckles and forearm. (Be careful if you have long fingernails that you don't dig them into your palms. An alternative method is to press the flat inner part of the finger tips against the base of the thumb).
      Now straighten your arm as hard as you can, and feel the tension in the muscle in the back of your upper arm – the triceps.

   Relaxation
   Now let go, and relax your arms. Relax all the muscles and feel the tension ease away. Breathe evenly, and as you breathe out think of the word RELAX.

9. *Biceps*
   Again, at first this strategy may be carried out with each arm separately.

   Tension strategy
   Bend you arms at the elbows and try to touch your wrists to your shoulders. Hold this position. Feel the tension in the muscle in the front of your upper arm – the biceps.

   Relaxation
   Now let go and relax your arms.

10. *Stomach*

   Tension strategy
   Take a deep breath. Put your hands on your stomach and tense it as if it were about to be punched. Tighten your stomach muscles hard, and hold your breath.

   Relaxation
   Now let go of your stomach muscles as you breathe out and think of the word RELAX.

11. *Legs and feet*
   At first this strategy may be carried out with each leg separately.

   Tension strategy
   Straighten your legs from the hips. Push your heels towards the opposite wall and your big toe inwards towards your head. Push hard and this will produce rapid tension. Relax. Then do the opposite: straighten your legs and push the toes downwards as hard as you can.

   Relaxation
   Now let go. Relax all the muscles of your legs.

That was the last exercise. Continue to let all the muscles of your body unwind and relax. Go through your body with your eyes closed and check that all your muscles are relaxed. Pay special attention to the areas of your body that become particularly tense.

Finally, open your eyes and gaze at a spot on the ceiling until your eyelids become tired and heavy, and then let them close naturally. As you do so look towards the end of your nose, so that your eyes are focused when they shut. Then attend passively to your breathing and feel yourself becoming more and more relaxed.

It may help to visualize a pleasant scene. For example, imagine you are lying on a sunny beach and the sea is coming in and going out in time to your breathing. Or, imagine you are in a cool meadow lying under a tree with the branches moving in time to your breathing. Imagine the scene as vividly as you can and then use it as you relax. Enjoy this feeling for as long as you wish or have time to do so, then count backwards from 4, to yourself. Slowly open your eyes and become alert again.

It is important to give yourself the instruction to become alert. You may have relaxed yourself into a light hypnotic trance. Don't rush around afterwards to make up for lost time... try and retain the feeling of calm and relaxation for as long as you can.

Quick relaxation

After practising the full relaxation every day for several weeks you will be able to become deeply relaxed in shorter periods of time first by combining muscle groups, then by simply recalling the exercises. Instead of tensing and releasing one group of muscles at a time, combine the muscles into the following four groups:

1. Face and neck
2. Arms and hands
3. Chest, shoulders, back and stomach
4. Legs and feet.

Once you have done your exercises, don't forget to return in your mind to your pleasant spot and spend a few minutes there just letting go. Enjoy feeling calm, confident and relaxed.

Stage two: Relaxation by recall

Starting with your forehead go through all the muscle groups of your body in your mind. Pay attention to each one and remember how they felt when fully relaxed. Allow all the muscles to become more and more deeply relaxed. Keep your eyes closed and your breathing relaxed. Remember that what you are aiming for is a skill that you can use at any time. It has to become a skill that you carry around with you. It is possible to reach the stage where you can be deeply and completely relaxed in a minute or less. Use your pleasant scene as a cue.

Go back to it in your mind and stay there until you are calm, confident and relaxed.

Anxiety management Step-by-step

Once you have practised relaxing every day and you feel that you are able to relax completely, you can begin to use your imagination as an ally in overcoming your fears. Until now your imagination has probably been working against you, conjuring up terrors of serious illness, madness or social disgrace. Now it must become your friend as you begin slowly to work your way towards freedom from your fears. Let it help you attempt to do the things you fear little by little, and to do them first only in your imagination.

Target Ladder
10. Travelling alone on the underground to work
9. Travelling with friend on the underground to work
8. Travelling on bus to work alone
7. Travelling home from work alone
6. Ten minutes in crowded shopping centre
5. Going into crowded shopping centre and coming out again immediately
4. Going to local shops alone on Saturday
3. Going to local shops alone during the week
2. Going to local shops with my husband on Saturday
1. Going to local shops with my husband during the week.

For this step-by-step approach (technically known as systematic desensitisation), you will need to construct a target ladder. Begin with a ladder with ten rungs. Each rung will represent a step in your anxiety-management campaign from the least upsetting (1) to the most upsetting (10). On the bottom rung write down some activity or situation that makes you feel slightly anxious. Then continue up in order of difficulty. The steps you decide on must be specific. It is no good writing down something vague and open-ended such as 'going out'. It is important to write down exactly what your first step is going to be (see the example on previous page). For someone who is very severely agoraphobic and has been confined to the house, this first step might be 'walking to the garden gate and back again'. In this case, your second step might be 'walk to the garden gate, turn right and walk to the first lamp-post and back again'. These first steps may not in themselves get you anywhere near where you want to be. They are designed to build your confidence to tackle more difficult situations later on.

It is important not to think about the higher steps when you are at the bottom of the ladder. Thinking about the seemingly difficult steps ahead may put you off attempting the first one. What you need to realise is that this ladder is very different from a conventional ladder. *You do not have to climb up it.* As you practise each step, your anxiety decreases and the next step becomes only as difficult as the first one. Each time you complete a step, it is like sawing off the bottom rung. The next step becomes the bottom one and you never have to go beyond the bottom rung of the ladder.

Practice in imagination

When you have constructed your ladder, you can start to practice your first step in your imagination. Carry out the relaxation exercises and when you are deeply relaxed go through your first step in great detail in your mind. If you are walking to the corner shop try to visualise the whole scene – the houses you will pass, the pillar box on the opposite corner and any other details that you can recall. If you become anxious at any point, stop thinking about the stressful situation and see how quickly you can reduce your anxiety by breathing calmly and slowly and becoming relaxed again. Then continue with this first step in your imagination once again. Practise in this way until you feel able to attempt your first step in reality.

Anxiety management in the actual situation

It is a good idea to practise your first step several times until you feel confident enough to move on to the second step. You may not be able to get as far as you planned on the first occasion. Don't give up. Just make a note of where you got to so that you can monitor your progress. Most important of all, congratulate yourself on having got as far as you did. Yes! It is very important to praise your efforts. Don't put yourself down by saying that at one time you could do such things without giving them much thought. At the moment they are very difficult for you, and you deserve congratulations for having the courage to begin to tackle you problems.

Rewards

For many of you, just being able to begin to tackle some of the situations you have avoided for so long is a reward in itself. Nevertheless, building a reward system into your plan will help to reinforce each step of the way. Plan a small reward for yourself for each step completed successfully and promise yourself a larger reward for reaching the top of the ladder. The rewards do not have to cost money. An extra hour in bed or coffee with a friend are two possibilities that spring to mind.

Continuing up the ladder

Continue your progress up the ladder. Practise your next step in your imagination when you are deeply relaxed. When you are able to get through this step in your mind with no anxiety, try it out in the real situation. Choose a time when you are feeling as calm as you are able, and preferably immediately after a relaxation session. And don't forget your reward when you have achieved another rung.

Going too quickly

Often the first steps of the ladder are the most difficult to complete. As you practise, your fears will tend to lessen and your confidence return. At this point beware of becoming over-confident and attempting feats that are much too difficult. If you have a panic attack, you may reduce your hard-won confidence dramatically and find yourself near the bottom of the ladder again.

Setbacks

Do not be dismayed if you find that on some days your anxiety is higher than on other days and you cannot continue with your programme. Normal anxiety levels go up and down and most of us have our off days. The level of your anxiety may alter according to the time of the month, the time of the year, the state of your health and how much stress or tension you have been under. Thus, you may have a bad day, a bad week, or a bad month, but don't give up. Carry on with the relaxation and wait until you feel able to pick up where you left off.

It may be that as you progress up the ladder you will find that your original order of difficulty has changed. Steps that seemed quite easy initially may now seem more difficult and vice versa. If this is the case just rearrange your ladder.

One word of warning: as you improve, you may feel that it is unnecessary to practise the relaxation. This is a trap that many fall into as soon as they begin to feel calmer. But don't be fooled. It is better to be safe than sorry, and practising relaxation is a sure way of keeping yourself steady.

Getting stuck

If you find that you are stuck and cannot move up to the next step, try and find a halfway step. Ask a friend or one of the family to come with you part of the way, or walk ahead of you and wait for you to catch up, or meet you at your destination. Do this until you have enough confidence to try the next step alone.

Other ways of helping yourself to reach the next step are:

1. Carrying out the relaxation exercises immediately before you attempt the practice steps.
2. If you have been prescribed tranquillising drugs by your

doctor, try to take them when they will have the maximum effect.

Anticipatory anxiety

Many of you will have found that you can go out or carry out some other activities you fear so long as you do so on the spur of the moment. If you have to wait, anxiety has a chance to increase and when the time comes round you find you cannot force yourself into the situation, or if you do manage, you experience panicky thoughts or feelings. If this is the case, don't plan your moves too far ahead, and try to undertake journeys and shopping at times when you can avoid long queues for the bus or at the supermarket check-out.

Diary keeping

As before, in our clinic we ask our patients to keep a diary, or fill in diary sheets, giving details of their activities, and the amount of time spent on them. (See the diary sheet below.) If the activities involve travelling we ask them to give the

Sample Diary Sheet											
Date	Relaxation	Activity	Time Start/Finish	Anxiety 0-10	Met	Accompanied	Alone	On foot	Bus	Car	Train
28-6	✓	Walking to the corner shop and back	10am–10.30am	7				✓	✓		
29-6	✓	Walking to corner shop and back	2pm–2.30pm	6							
30-6	0	Walking to the end of parade of shops	2pm–3pm	6	✓			✓			

approximate distance. There are also columns giving information about whether they were on their own or had someone with them, what type of transport was used, and whether relaxation was carried out prior to the activity. In addition we ask them to rate the level of their anxiety on a scale 0–10 so that they can measure the depth of the fear they feel during their practice and judge how much their anxiety level rises or falls. It is very important to gauge your feelings accurately in this way so that you have not only a measure of your success but a guide as to when to move on to the next step. Once you are able to keep your anxiety below 5 (or 50 per cent) you can start a new step.

In this way both patient and therapist can build a picture of the range of difficulty involved and adjust the target ladder if necessary. At the same time we have a record of progress. This record is crucial because small successes are very easily forgotten and setbacks are often magnified. Diary keeping helps you to maintain a more balanced view of your progress.

Flooding

As the name suggests, flooding is the opposite of the step-by-step approach. I would strongly recommend, therefore, that you do not attempt this method on a self-help basis but seek the help of a clinical psychologist. Nevertheless, I will give you a sketch of the procedure so that you know what to expect. It is an approach that is speedy and effective but it must be used with caution. Flooding is similar to jumping into the deep end of the swimming pool rather than inching your way down the steps, gingerly testing the coldness of the water. It involves experiencing your worst fears in reality – and all at once.

Your worst fears will be those at the top of your target ladder. Your top step might be travelling on a bus or train at the height of the rush hour. Using the flooding approach you plunge straight into the feared situation and stay in it until your anxiety level returns to normal. You will probably need to repeat the procedure two or three times until you feel comfortable in the situation. It is important to understand that, although the effects of anxiety can be uncomfortable and unpleasant, anxiety cannot harm you physically or mentally. You may be flooded with anxiety but you will not drown. Your anxiety level will always come down, and it will come down in a predictable way. They only contra-indications for flooding are abnormal physical conditions such as heart disease or high blood pressure. If you are in any doubt about your health in this respect, check with your doctor first.

Anxiety Curves

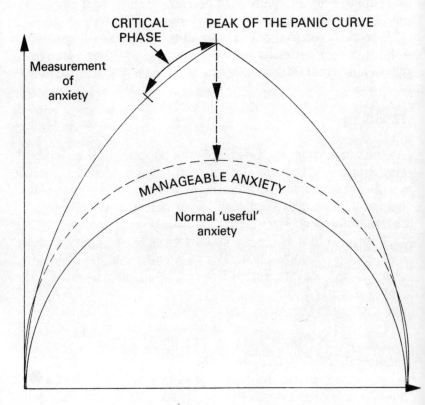

Time in minutes

The anxiety curve

The easiest way to illustrate what will happen when you take the plunge is with a diagram (see previous page) which shows the 'curve' of a person's anxiety. As you enter the feared situation your anxiety increases. The lowest curve on the diagram represents normal 'useful' anxiety, which is a response to actual danger. The body gears itself up for fighting or fleeing. This is its survival mechanism. The curve above, drawn with a broken line, represents manageable anxiety. By employing techniques such as deep breathing, relaxation and positive self-talk, you can prevent your anxiety going on to the panic curve at the top. If you have already reached that peak, you can still talk yourself down. The portion of the curve marked *critical phase* is the time when you are most highly aroused. If you decide to leave the anxiety-making situation at this point, you will feel an immediate relief. But next time you try to approach the same or a similar situation you may not be able to face up to it and that is the danger. Also, you know that you have 'opted out' and have deprived yourself of the chance to establish the basis of real confidence in managing your fears. In other words, you may feel that you have let yourself down. More important you have not given yourself the opportunity to enjoy the tremendous elation and surge of confidence that comes after you have tackled your phobia.

Staying where you are

If you accept the unpleasant feelings and stay where you are then your anxiety will inevitably drop. You can speed up this process by breathing correctly and going through the 'coping thoughts' which I talked about in Chapter 2. Remember that your fear reactions are kept going by your alarming thoughts.

If you feel that you really cannot stay where you are and you are in, for example, a supermarket, the best thing to do is to run out and around the block and come back in again.

Taking a relaxed attitude

It is said to be a British characteristic to face problems with grit, stiff upper lip and grim determination. All of these aspects of stoicism have their place in life but not in a programme for managing fears, phobias and panics.

Yes, you do have to begin to face your problems. You do have to accept, in measured doses, the unpleasant symptoms of anxiety. You do have to face the worst that could happen to you and you do have to persevere. What you do not have to do is to make your therapy programme into a battle-plan and fight your way through. The moment you start to fight, your muscles will become tense, your breathing becomes rapid and shallow and you will be well on the way to experiencing all the physical symptoms you are trying to avoid.

The key to your self-help programme is relaxation, and maintaining a relaxed attitude so that you can relax your way through situations that you fear. If you believe that you have to fight and fight, you will end up feeling tired and dispirited. Carry on with your practice when you feel relaxed and optimistic. If you feel too anxious to do anything unpleasant, stay at home and start again the next day.

It is particularly important when you are attempting to overcome your fears not to dwell on failure. If you have tried you have not failed. Little by little you are moving towards your goal of overcoming your phobic *habits*.

With the help of family and friends

'If the medicine is to do you any good it must be unpleasant' may be one of the unhelpful attitudes that was instilled in you in childhood. Your parents may have taught you to struggle with your problems. They may have implied that having fears and anxieties was not grown-up or not manly. You may have been taught to:

'Keep your feelings to yourself'

'Don't let yourself down'
'Show a brave face to the world'.

As a result of this conditioning you may feel that talking to
others about your fears is embarrassing or even dangerous. It
is time to reconsider these beliefs as they may be working
against you. Your parents were not always right and family
sayings such as these may have to be dumped in the dustbin.
Instead, tell your family and friends about your fears and ask
for help. You will, I'm sure, discover that most people have at
some time had experiences similar to your own.

Try to involve a friend or member of your family in your self-
help programme so that you have an ally standing by or at the
end of a telephone to give you encouragement, share your
disappointment over setbacks and rejoice with you when you
are successful. You need someone to talk to on the days when
you feel like giving up and retreating from the world. Ask your
family and friends to read the next chapter which is intended
especially for them.

A word of warning

If you are seeking to treat yourself, you will naturally seek the
help of those closest to you. You do need help but you do not
need *any* help, and most of all you do not need kindly meant but
unhelpful help. You will have to be very honest with yourself,
and avoid leaning on those who offer themselves as a crutch
instead of offering you encouragement to walk on your own
two feet. There is no need to be suspicious of a loving and
helpful partner who likes your company and will do anything
for you. Simply remember that it is better for you if you are
able to manage on your own. If your partner truly cares for
you, he or she will support you every inch of the way. You must
make sure that you do not take advantage of that and lean too
heavily.

Beware of false friends

Another trap that you might fall into is accepting the

reassurance of so-called 'friends' with the same problem. These are people who have found that their phobia, however unpleasant, protects them from situations and conflicts that they would rather not confront. Their lives may be limited and not very satisfying but they feel this is preferable to facing their fears. That is their choice. You need to beware of 'support' from those people who have settled into a phobic life-style and are more or less content to stay that way. They may want to recruit new members for their way of life and will no doubt be happy to discuss their symptoms and your symptoms for ever and a day. They will discourage rather than encourage you to lead a normal life so avoid them if you can. Just as their phobia is a false friend, so they will be a false friend to you.

CHAPTER 4

Your Family and Friends

If a member of your family or a close friend is suffering from fears, phobias or panic attacks, you are inevitably affected. Seeing anyone suffer is unpleasant and can make you feel helpless and inadequate. Feeling incapable of helping a loved one overcome their problems can be frustrating, and living with someone who is incapable of carrying out simple, every-day activities can be exasperating.

Helping someone to overcome their phobic problems and return to a normal way of life requires patience and real understanding. This chapter tells you how you can best support and encourage an anxious or phobic relative or friend. It offers practical advice and guidance as to what kind of help is needed. Often, from the best of motives, family and friends give the wrong kind of help. For example, they may be over-helpful. They may even unwittingly have contributed to the state the sufferer is in. Or, without realising it, they may have a vested interest in maintaining the situation. You, as well as the sufferer, need to understand the underlying problems not just the goals of treatment. (For the rest of the chapter I shall talk about 'your partner' to cover all possible relationships with the phobic person, and for convenience I shall use the pronoun 'her'.)

What lies behind the anxiety?

By now your partner may have a conditioned fear reaction to certain situations and she will need your help to begin to learn how to manage her anxiety. Before discussing what you can do to help in this endeavour, it is crucial that you investigate whether or not there is an underlying problem which has not been recognised. If you are a close partner, it is vital that you give some thought to possible problems, conflicts or grievances that may have given rise to your partner's fears.

In clinical practice, many patients come for treatment of anxiety or panic which they have defined as *the* problem. More often than not, however, the phobia is the surface manifestation of an unresolved conflict. Perhaps there is a conflict that neither of you has been able to resolve or a decision to be made that you cannot agree upon. It may be that your partner would like to start a family and you feel trapped at the thought of having children, or your partner would like to start a business and you are terrified of the financial risk. Your partner may be unhappy in the marriage but is too unassertive to say how she feels. If you concentrate your efforts on helping your partner to confront her fears about going out (or whatever her superficial fear is), you will be addressing the symptoms and not the cause. The underlying problem will remain untouched and she will continue to have symptoms of one kind or another. If the underlying cause is marital disharmony, you may need marriage guidance counselling. You can arrange for this yourself by telephoning your local Relate (Marriage Guidance Council) Office.

Her problem, or yours?

It may be that the underlying problem has been resolved but your partner is left with a conditioned fear response and avoidance habit. If your partner has been unable to get over her problems, even when the underlying cause is known, it is possible that it is you and your 'kindness' that is the stumbling block. You may be preventing your phobic partner from recovering by providing too much help and support. The 'golden' partner is the one who does everything for the phobic without complaint and with a great deal of emotional support. While kindness and helpfulness are very valuable commodities, in the case of phobics they may need to be restricted.

Restricting the amount of help may be difficult for some partners because of their own needs. It may be necessary to look long and hard at what motivates you. Ask yourself if your own difficulties in childhood have made you very anxious about separation and about being alone. If the answer is Yes, it may be that having a wife, husband or partner reliably at home increases your own feeling of security. Your own fears may be hindering your partner's recovery.

An example of how this type of problem comes about may be helpful. After several years of agoraphobia, Sylvia came for treatment and we discovered that her problem was being maintained, unwittingly, by her husband, Geoff. Geoff had had a very insecure childhood. When he was 3 his mother had had to spend four months in hospital and Geoff had been cared for by a variety of neighbours and friends. When he was 7, Geoff's father had gone off with another woman. His mother was forced to take a full-time job so that the now fatherless Geoff came home to an empty house. Geoff married Sylvia knowing that she was rather nervous of being on her own or travelling far from home. Without realising it, Geoff encouraged the nervous habit. He took the children to school, did the shopping, walked the dog. Sylvia went out less and less. Geoff was only being kind, but his kindness brought him advantages that he unconsciously yearned for – a woman who was always at home when he returned.

Self-esteem

One of the possible spin-offs from having a partner who is phobic is that you can maintain a high level of self-esteem by contrasting yourself with your phobic partner. In clinical practice we sometimes find that the well partner becomes extremely anxious when the 'sick' partner starts to get better. It seems that the anxiety has to be carried by one partner or the other. Again, it is crucial that the underlying problems are explored and you may need professional help in doing so. Meanwhile, you can do a lot to help your partner to overcome the phobic habit.

Fading out the help

Our usual response to suffering is a desire to help. Unfortunately, too much help may strengthen the phobic habit. Each time that you offer to go out and do the shopping or stay at home with the anxious person, the discomfort of the moment is removed.

During phases of acute anxiety, this kind of attentive kindness is crucial. Later on, your kindly help can be used in another way as you encourage your partner to do more and more on her own and face the situation she fears. This may mean that you have to forego your own unrecognised satisfaction in having your partner totally dependent on you. As she gains confidence you should fade out the help. It is like teaching a child to swim or ride a bicycle. At a certain stage you have to allow them to go forward on their own. If they know you are standing by in case they get into difficulties, their anxiety will be lessened. Unlike someone who is confident enough to strike out alone, the sufferer may be terrified of letting go of your hand. Once you are sure that she can manage, it is kinder to let go, even if you find it hard to stand by and watch her struggle. Both too little care and too much protection are counter-productive. What you are trying to achieve is the right balance between caring and protection. This is what is meant by 'tough love'. If you gradually fade out your help it will lessen the difficulty for both of you, and heighten the pleasure when your partner achieves her goal.

Running out of patience

Of course your difficulty may not be that you are too sympathetic to your partner. It may be the opposite. You may be totally fed up with having to cope with a phobic partner. It can feel like a very long and thankless task. This is particularly so if you are having to deal with what is known as *anticipatory anxiety*. That is to say, when your partner's anxiety is low, you will find that she will promise to go to a party or other event and then, as the time comes near, will begin to experience anxiety or even terror. She finds when the moment arrives that, however much she wants to do what has been planned, she cannot do it. In your disappointment, you may begin to lose your patience and tell the sufferer to pull herself together. But that will only make things worse. No doubt your partner has tried, and is still trying, to pull herself together and has failed. If it were that easy to pull herself together she would have done so by now. She has no doubt disappointed herself as well as you, and will be feeling a miserable failure.

It is far more effective to encourage your partner to relax and to provide her with the possibility of leaving the feared situation easily. With this sort of reassurance about an escape route, she may be able to overcome her fear sufficiently to enable her to do *part* of what was planned. If it is a social event you could telephone in advance and say that you can only stay for a short time. Otherwise just leave your partner at home without making a fuss, and do not feel that you have to stay with her unless she insists. Many phobic people feel enormous guilt about letting everyone down and the guilt will be increased if she feels that she has spoiled your day.

Emotional blackmail

Sadly, some phobics consciously or unconsciously use their inability to go out or to remain alone as a way of keeping those around them bound to them. Do not immediately withdraw your sympathy and understanding if you think you are being manipulated in this way. Your partner may be quite unaware of how she is using her difficulties to imprison you, and if she is aware of what she is doing it is a measure of how desperate or hopeless she feels about maintaining a relationship on any other basis. Decide that in future you will reassure her of your love and support but be firm about what you are prepared to offer in the way of help. Try to encourage and motivate your partner to be less dependent on you and to widen the network of support. Get her to confide in friends or other members of the family, or even better get her to seek professional help.

Depression

If your partner is seriously depressed, it is not the time to start tackling her phobic problems. As a first step, your partner should be persuaded to consult her doctor. Often phobic problems are related to depression and will disappear as the *mood state* improves. If depression is not too severe you can help motivate your partner to follow the self-help advice for dealing with depression outlined in Chapter 2.

Children

Often children are bewildered and become anxious themselves when they see a parent in a distressed state. You can help by explaining to the child what is going on, even if you have to admit that you do not understand why your partner has these problems. Children react very badly to being 'fobbed off' with a false explanation but they can stand being told that you do not understand. A child will also quickly become used to a parent always being at home and may well feel insecure if the parent begins to behave differently. They may be quite distressed when he or she goes out and will need some extra reassurance. You can help by explaining that it is good for mummy to go out on her own and that the child is not being abandoned.

Helping with the therapy programme

In Chapters 2 and 3 I outlined a cognitive–behaviour programme with two main behavioural methods of helping phobic patients to overcome their difficulties and manage their anxiety: a step-by-step approach and a flooding approach. The latter is the quicker, more effective way of overcoming fear but is not a method to be used on a self-help basis. If your partner is willing to try this short, sometimes unpleasant treatment, then I would strongly recommend that she does so only under the care of a clinical psychologist or psychiatrist experienced in this technique. Apart from their lack of experience, particularly in gauging levels of anxiety, family and friends are usually too emotionally involved to maintain the clinical objectivity necessary to carry out this particular technique. The following clinical example is to give you a picture of the way the treatment is carried out so that you understand what is happening (further examples are given in Chapter 5). Your role – and a very important one – will be to offer your partner encouragement and support to face her fear and to go through with it.

Taking the plunge

Marjorie was a patient of mine who decided to take the plunge. She had always feared going out by herself, but had been surrounded by family and friends who bolstered her confidence in undertaking the numerous social engagements that were part of her daily life as a diplomat's wife. Suddenly her husband was given a new posting – they were to move to a city where she would know nobody, and where she would often be left on her own, and have to go out on her own. She would also have to manage large gatherings of people. Marjorie's worst fear was of finding herself alone in a crowd. She was even nervous of going shopping, though she knew she had lots of things to buy for her new life.

This was an ideal opportunity for flooding. We decided that she should spend three mornings at a local shopping centre. Both of us found the first morning rather exhausting. Marjorie started well, got into a shop, chose some items, but in the end put down her basket before she reached the till and fled back to me. With more encouragement from me, she tackled another shop, and this time managed to buy some lightweight shirts for her husband. But she was extremely tired by the time she finished.

On day two, Marjorie succeeded in buying some clothes for herself, and visited two more shops before finding me again and being rewarded with a relaxing cup of coffee. We were both proud of her achievement. It had not been easy. On day three Marjorie was still nervous, but this time she knew that she could and would manage her anxiety. The worst was over. Marjorie's fear had not disappeared entirely, she was worn out by the tension she had experienced, but she had won. She knew that her fear was manageable.

If your partner opts for the flooding method, remember Marjorie. Your first response should be tremendous encouragement for her bravery and a reminder that this method has a long history of success. Try to be there when she returns from her practice sessions. If she has not been able to face her fears, then encourage her to try again. Help her to be confident that if she goes into the situation she fears and stays there her anxiety will definitely lessen and she will be able to manage – phobic anxiety always comes down. Emphasise that the first part of the treatment is the worst and that the worst will soon be over. Taking the plunge will be a reward in itself, but sometimes a special gift in recognition of her courage will enhance her sense of achievement.

Step-by-step approach

This is a procedure that I can recommend on a self-help basis. Where time is not an important factor, a step-by-step approach is a treatment you can tackle together.

If your partner is very tense, as a first step she will need to find a way of relaxing. Many couples enjoy learning to relax together. Follow the programme outlined in the previous chapter, or make or buy a relaxation tape and practice together. If you have a tense partner, she is bound to make you tense too. If doing the relaxation exercises makes your partner more tense (and this can happen), plan an alternative programme. Any exercise will reduce tension, and playing tennis, swimming, dancing, yoga or aerobics will give you a lot of enjoyment as well as making you fit. You may even want to join a sports club where you will meet like-minded people.

The target ladder

In our therapy programme we ask our patients to prepare a target ladder. This is something you can help with. The ladder is a series of steps that your partner is going to take, from the easiest to the most difficult. You can help her to find and grade a series of target situations. (There is an example on page 72.) As an observer, you may be more aware of the situations that she avoids and can help her to select the right steps – the ones that are manageable with a little effort but not too much. Once the programme is under way you may be able to make useful suggestions for halfway steps if you feel that some of the situations are too far apart in terms of difficulty. Please remember, however, that your partner knows best what situations are difficult for her, so allow her to have the final say. And don't forget that too much help is as bad as too little. You can hold the ladder but your partner must climb it alone. Your job is to accompany her climb with rung-by-rung encouragement to achieve, and praise for each achievement.

Getting going

Your partner may have read this book, taught herself to relax, practised being in the first situation on her ladder in her imagination and be waiting for the right moment to start putting her self-help programme into operation. This is where you come in. She needs to be encouraged to start *now*.

Once you have persuaded your partner to take the first step, you can be on hand to congratulate her on her efforts or to encourage her to try again if her courage fails at her first attempt. Praise is not only more pleasant but is far more effective in changing behaviour for the better than criticism, so please remember to praise your partner's efforts. Do not forget more tangible rewards. What you are aiming for is a link between the phobic activity or situation and something pleasant. The practice sessions will be much more effective if there is something pleasant waiting for her at the end of, say, a shopping trip, or a bus journey, or spending time on her own at home. Plan the reward whatever it is – a bunch of flowers, a meal in a restaurant, or a cup of coffee – as close in time as possible to the successful completion of one of the steps.

Thoughts and mental pictures

Obviously you will wish to listen sympathetically to the feelings that are aroused during your partner's practice sessions but try to avoid encouraging a constant repetition of upsetting thoughts and feelings. Instead, concentrate on the cognitive aspect of the treatment programme. (The word cognitive covers the thoughts, mental pictures and belief system that are important elements in the phobic habit.) Often the thoughts that trigger panicky feelings are quite automatic and it may take a lot of hard work and attention to catch them. Once you have helped to catch them try to offer alternative thoughts or better still encourage your partner to generate more useful thoughts. The way to do this is to ask questions of the 'Could you be feeling like this because . . . ?' type. In this way you can help her to argue with her negative thoughts and beliefs.

There are certain negative thoughts that seem to arise as soon as a person starts to practise and which are common to many phobics. These negative thoughts have to be attacked otherwise they will undermine your partner's efforts. Here are some examples of the thoughts that phobics have, the questions you can put and the possible alternative thoughts.

1. **Negative thought:** 'I did not manage to stay in the cinema. I'm obviously too ill to try.'
    Question: 'Were you able to stay in the cinema for five or ten minutes?'
    Alternative thought: 'Yes. I made a start and I will try to go back again as soon as I have the time.'

2. **Negative thought:** 'When I looked at my diary for the week, I thought: "I used to be able to do all these things without thinking about them."'

Question:	'Yes, that is true, but were you anxious at the time?'
Alternative thought:	'I did very well this week when I consider how anxious I was.'

3.   **Negative thought:** 'Going to the hairdresser isn't anything to be pleased about, anyone could do it.'

Question:	'Would anyone be able to sit under the dryer for half an hour feeling as you do?'
Alternative thought:	'Anyone else would have had difficulty in staying there if they had felt as trapped and self-conscious as I did.'

The reason why it is so crucial to get hold of the unreasonable thoughts is that they create tension, anxiety, depression and loss of confidence. To the phobic person, these negative thoughts seem to be quite reasonable. Consequently, it is extremely difficult for them to argue with the thoughts when they try to do this alone. When the phobic person has a bad day, she may feel so hopeless or so aroused that the setback is magnified and her responses are quite unrealistic. She will need your help to track down the NATS (negative automatic thoughts) and substitute more helpful positive automatic thoughts (PATS). She does not have to believe the alternative thoughts completely. It may be that all you can do is introduce a certain amount of doubt into her mind as to the validity of her thoughts and assumptions.

Helping with the practice

Early on in her recovery programme, especially if she is working alone, you may be needed to accompany your partner on her practice sessions. She may want you to go with her for part of the way or to meet her half way. Later on, your assistance may be needed to tackle more difficult steps such as bus or train journeys. Here you can help by meeting your partner at a certain bus stop or sitting upstairs on the bus whilst she sits downstairs. If sitting in a cinema or theatre is difficult for her, you can help her to find a seat at the end of the row so that she does not feel too trapped.

Panic attacks

You may already be thinking 'What on earth should I do if she has a panic attack.' If you can manage it, try to persuade her to stay where she is until the anxiety subsides, which it will, I promise you. Persuading her to stay may not be possible as, in her terror, she may have bolted, either out of the supermarket or off the bus. In which case, stay with her; wait until she is feeling less anxious and help her to try again.

I know from my own experience how helpful this sort of encouragement and practical help can be. Once, leaving a hospital in one of the home counties, I was involved in a very serious accident. An hour after it happened, two kindly policemen insisted that I drive my car as slowly as I liked with one of them sitting beside me and one behind. Driving my car was the last thing I wanted to do but they persuaded me that it was essential that I start to drive as soon as possible. I had to drive 6 miles to where I was staying and I drove at about 10 miles an hour. During that time the policeman beside me gently encouraged me to go on. At the end of the journey he explained to me that he was anxious to ensure that I did not develop a phobia of driving. Not content with this first journey, he told me that they would be happy to call again the following morning and accompany me on my journey to the hospital. I accepted gladly and with their help gradually regained my confidence in driving.

Exhaustion

Being in a constant state of tension is very tiring. It is the equivalent of carrying a heavy load about all day. If your partner practices relaxation regularly, this load will lighten. Nevertheless, in the early stages of practice she may tire quite easily.

Another reason why many phobics tire easily is that they have been more or less housebound for many months and so have not had much practice in walking. Paul, a music student, found that he was exhausted when he attempted even quite short walks. You can read an account of his problems and treatment in Chapter 5. At first he was convinced that his breathlessness, pounding heart and trembling legs were signs that he was seriously ill with a heart condition. After a thorough physical examination by his doctor, and further tests, he realised that he was out of condition and needed to improve his stamina. This lack of stamina and his tendency to suffer hypoglycaemic (low blood sugar) attacks had led him to believe that he might die at any moment.

Panic attacks and low blood sugar

Paul was diagnosed as having low blood sugar (hypogly-caemia) after he fainted during a weekend concert tour. This hypoglycaemic attack was associated with not having eaten during the day. Subsequently, when he found himself in a similar situation to the one in which he had this experience, he had a real panic attack. Make sure, therefore, that your partner pays attention to her diet and does not go without meals and particularly breakfast. Fashions in so-called healthy eating change dramatically so I will not add to the general confusion about food by advocating special diets. As in all things, it is a matter of getting the right balance and eating food that is as close as possible to its natural state.

It is sensible, however, if your partner is subject to low blood sugar attacks, to make sure that she does not have too many sweet snacks. Many people make the mistake of assuming that if blood sugar is low the first thing they should do is to eat some sugar. Sweet snacks that give a sudden boost in blood glucose levels such as cakes, biscuits, sweets, jams, chocolate or high sugar content drinks should be avoided. Try to replace these sugary foods with carbohydrates in their natural form: bread, pasta, potatoes and rice give a slower, more even release of energy – and they contain vitamins too.

Alcohol

Your partner may feel that alcohol will give her courage. If she is taking medicines for anxiety or depression, do remind her that alcohol and medicine should not be mixed. Even if she is not taking drugs remember that alcohol is a sedative. It will make you feel good for a while, but miserable if you drink too much. If your partner is feeling low or anxious, a cup of tea or a hot milky drink will be infinitely better for her.

Doing things slowly and calmly

One of the reasons why Paul was experiencing alarming symptoms early on in his practice was that he was still breathing too quickly – in fact he was doing everything too quickly. It was noticeable when he was talking to me that his words were tumbling out and the room was full of tension. This is where you can be of great assistance. Encourage your partner to slow down. Get her to walk and talk slowly and to remain relaxed. When you are with her during her practice try to avoid any anxiety-provoking subjects and instead involve her in talking about something that interests her or amuses her. Laughter is a sure sign of a relaxed mood. In this way, you will distract her from upsetting thoughts and feelings.

There are times when distraction is the only way to deal with fear. I remember some years ago being traumatised as a passenger in a car when I realised that we were travelling down a spiral mountain road on the outside edge. I began to feel quite panic-stricken. My sister who was driving the car and who is an editor of children's books began to tell me a fascinating fairy story about a princess and a unicorn. Although I was well past the age to be told fairy stories, I was astonished to find myself gradually drawn into the story and the journey down seemed only a matter of minutes. Obviously, you are going to attract a lot of attention if you start telling your partner fairy stories in the middle of a crowded supermarket. It is up to you to use your creativity to find a way of keeping your partner absorbed and her anxiety at bay.

What not to do

Whatever you do, do not draw your partner's attention to her symptoms by asking questions such as: 'Are you all right?'; 'Are you going to be able to manage?'; 'You're not going to have one of your funny turns, are you?' For all you know, your partner may be calmly enjoying what she is doing and your questions will trigger the habitual anxiety response. It is also unpleasant for an adult to be treated like a child. It is bad enough feeling like one. So do your best to bolster your partner's self-esteem.

Varying the practice steps

Another way in which you can be creative is to help your partner to vary the way in which she carries out the practice items. A walk in town on Saturday will be a very different experience from a quiet Sunday walk when not too many people are about. You may even find that you can suggest variations in the practice item on the spur of the moment before she has time to build up anxiety. As you are no doubt aware, phobics are often able to do things on the spur of the moment when they do not have time to anticipate all the possible terrors.

Diary keeping

In our clinic, we ask patients to keep a diary of their daily activities and these are discussed at weekly or fortnightly intervals. If your partner is working without a professional therapist, she may find it helpful to show you her diary. Discuss this with her and find out if she feels it would be helpful. In this way, particularly in the later stages when you have faded out your physical presence, you will be kept up to date with where your partner is on her ladder.

Sticking points

It may be that your partner will settle at a certain point and not wish to continue up the ladder. In my experience, many people reach a stage where they can do most of what they want to achieve and are feeling a great deal better. At this point, they stick for fear of rocking the ladder. They fear that if they attempt the more difficult rungs of the ladder, whether this is travelling on the underground or going on holiday, they may find themselves back at the bottom. This is when reassurance is needed. They need to be reassured that they will not go back to rung one because they are now different people. They have learned a great deal about themselves. They know about their bodily reactions; they know about their negative automatic thoughts (the NATS) and how these give rise to anxious and depressed feelings. They have learned how to manage their anxiety. They need to hear someone say all this to them and to encourage them to carry on with the good work. Do not be afraid to take the initiative if you think this is what is going on and suggest that it might be time to move up a rung.

If you find that your partner's self-help programme is getting nowhere, getting her down or getting you down, you probably need to seek help elsewhere. Help from a professional is never a bad idea. Just as some people are good at do-it-yourself home improvement, others are not. You may be a natural therapist but if you are not, find somebody who is able to help. If your partner likes the idea of the two-pronged cognitive–behaviour approach I have outlined, then she should ask her doctor if he can put her in touch with a clinical psychologist who is qualified in the technique.

CHAPTER 5

Professional Help

Those of you who are suffering from phobias or panic attacks may be apprehensive about the whole idea of seeking professional help. How do you set about it? How do you find the right clinic? What is involved in professional treatment? The answer to the first two questions is to approach your doctor and ask for a referral to the clinical psychology department of your local hospital or to a clinical psychologist in private practice. In answer to the last question, I hope that this book has helped you to begin to understand your difficulties at a deeper level as well as guiding you in the methods used to overcome or manage the phobic habits which tend to be seen as the main problem. In order to give you some idea of what is involved in professional treatment, I am including some clinical conversations composed from typical therapeutic sessions with men and women (aged 19–75) who have been referred for help with their problems. The names and personal details are fictitious.

How long does professional therapy take?

This may well be your next question as it is one that I am often asked. I am afraid that there is no simple answer. The nature and degree of people's problems vary considerably, so, although the basic approach will be similar, therapy will be tailored to suit the individual; consequently the period of treatment will vary in length from person to person. It may take only two or three weeks, or it may take two years. Often the initial symptoms of anxiety, avoidance and panic disappear quite quickly and the person feels greatly relieved. Unfortunately, the relief is often accompanied by a fear of doing anything that might 'rock the ladder'. The person is grateful to be able to lead a normal life – going to work and going out without fear – but is wary of undertaking any major change such as a new job, moving house, starting a new relationship. Although they feel better, they still need help. That is why we spend time working on the underlying causes of these conditions, and looking at the individual's whole life.

What will happen?

I hope that the conversations that follow will give some idea of what to expect if you decide to seek treatment. You will find that the patients who are describing their difficulties and learning to manage them are people like yourselves with similar problems. You may even recognise yourself in some of these situations. As you will see, the problems and their roots are all different yet the sufferers share similar feelings and reactions. You will see how the therapist looks at what has been going on in your life, assesses your symptoms, decides with you on the best approach to your treatment, helps uncover hidden feelings and conflicts, and teaches you how to change unhelpful thoughts and beliefs. In practice, a full assessment of the person's problems would be carried out; here there is only room to give fragments of longer, in-depth conversations. I hope, however, that these will give you an idea of the process of the therapeutic work and will encourage you to seek professional help if necessary.

Good luck with your treatment, whether it is on your own, with the help of family or friends, or with a therapist (referred to as Psychol: in the conversations).

Conversations

SUSAN: aged 36, wife and mother of two children, aged 10 and 11.

Psychol:	Perhaps you would begin by telling me when your problems started.
Susan:	It was after our holiday in July when I thought that I was feeling much better. I had been under a lot of stress because my husband Jack had been quite seriously ill and had to undergo major surgery in June. He is back at work now but I still worry about him. I was shopping locally and suddenly it hit me. I felt sick and dizzy and thought I was going to faint.
Psychol:	What did you do?
Susan:	I had to get out of the shop. I was trembling all over and I just left the packages on the counter and rushed out. I don't know how I managed to get home.
Psychol:	When did you begin to feel better?
Susan:	As I got nearer my house, but I still felt very shaky for hours afterwards.
Psychol:	Can you remember what sort of thoughts were going through your mind when you began to get these feelings?
Susan:	I was sure that everyone could see that I was sweating and trembling. I felt that I was the centre of attention and I just wanted to get away from all those eyes.
Psychol:	Were you able to do your shopping the next time?
Susan:	The next day I thought I must do some shopping but I got as far as the row of shops and those feelings started to come back and I was scared to death. I felt as if my feet wouldn't move and I couldn't force myself to go any further. I had never been like that before and it was worse the next day. I found that I was too frightened to go out. My

sister-in-law lives nearby and she has been extremely helpful. She's been doing my shopping for me and she comes with me in the car when I go to pick up the children from school. Driving the car is fine so long as I have someone with me but I can't go out alone.

Psychol: I am wondering if there were times when your husband was so ill that you thought he might die and you would be left on your own.

Susan: Yes. And now, even though he's a great deal better, I often think how would I cope if he died. I have never been one for being on my own. When my mother was alive, we used to do everything together. She died five years ago and I thought I would go to pieces. My son was only a year old so I suppose I had to keep going.

Psychol: It seems that you coped with your husband's illness for many months and that you kept going but now he is so much better you are aware of feeling unsafe.

Susan: Yes. I feel just like a child. In fact my young son offered to take me to the shops at the weekend.

Psychol: It is clear that your sense of security has been undermined by your husband's illness. Your sister-in-law and now your son are attempting to provide substitute support.

Susan: Yes. I realise now that I have always been very dependent on someone. Really I blame my mother for that because she was over-protective.

Psychol: Fortunately, it is possible to develop a sense of safety by various coping methods such as learning to relax and making changes in the way in which you think and talk to yourself.

Susan: At the moment my thoughts are all about possible dangers.

Psychol: In your case it seems that you rely for support on just one or two people. Perhaps as a long-term goal we can look at some ways of establishing a wider support system. Meanwhile our short-term goal will be to help you to feel safer and then to practise going out by yourself and I will explain the procedure to you.

LINDA: aged 22, a computer programmer

Psychol: Could you tell me in your own words what has brought you for psychological help?

Linda: Yes. I have been very panicky over the last year and I have tried everything. I don't know if I can get any help from anyone but I thought it was worth a try. My doctor suggested that I should come and see you. I don't expect the attacks to go away but I would like to know if there is some way I can cope with them more easily.

Psychol: Do the panicky feelings come and go at certain times?

Linda: Yes. Mostly they happen when I am by myself and when I am driving the car but now they are even happening when I am with other people.

Psychol: Could you tell me how often they happen?

Linda: Every day, just about every day.

Psychol: Can you describe the last attack you had?

Linda: Yes. It was yesterday evening. I was in my car at about 6 o'clock, driving myself back to the flat from Surrey. Suddenly I started breathing very quickly and feeling giddy. My hands went numb and I felt very churned up inside as if I was going to faint. Last night's attack was really bad. I had to pull over and stop the car and get out and lean against the car. I thought I was going to faint.

Psychol: And then?

Linda: After a while, I managed to get back in my car and I just drove to a friend's house. I barged in. She must have thought I was mad because I could barely speak but I was past caring what anyone thought of me.

Psychol: Do you have any clues as to why you might have started to feel panicky over the past year?

Linda: Well, the attacks often happen when I am by myself and I think maybe they are a reaction to being on my own. I feel quite lonely living in London.

Psychol: Is there anything that helps you feel better?

Linda: A friend of mine said that breathing into a paper bag would help once it's started so I always carry a paper bag with me. Sometimes when I feel my breathing getting very fast, I breathe into the bag. But I can't do that at the office and when I'm driving. People would think that I was really odd.

Psychol: And does it seem to help?

Linda: Yes, it helps in that the panic doesn't get worse but it doesn't stop the attack coming on. Sometimes if I can breathe more slowly I can stop the panic from getting worse.

Psychol: Can you think of anything that seems to trigger it off? Can you detect any pattern of these attacks?

Linda: No. As I say they seem to happen when I am alone or know that I am going to be alone.

Psychol: When you are on your own, do you feel nervous and insecure?

Linda: Yes. In a way I suppose I'm homesick. I'm just not used to a big city.

Psychol: You mentioned earlier that these attacks are now happening even when you are with other people.

Linda: Oh yes, they are happening when other people are around and that really alarms me. I'm frightened that they will think I'm mad. It has happened even when I have been with my friends. They try to be sympathetic and understanding but it's very embarrassing. They don't know what to do and they keep telling me not to worry.

Psychol: Has anyone explained to you that you are overbreathing and that this is common in people who are chronically anxious.

Linda:	My friend said that I was hyperventilating.
Psychol:	Yes, you mentioned using a paper bag and I wonder if your friend explained to you why this can be helpful.
Linda:	Not really. I was so desperate I just took her advice. I didn't stop to ask why it worked.
Psychol:	Put quite simply, when you over breathe (hyperventilate) you blow out a lot of carbon-dioxide. This has an effect on the chemistry of the body and you get the sort of reactions you have just described. One way of dealing with over breathing once it has started is to put a paper bag over your nose and mouth and in this way you take in some of the carbon dioxide that you have breathed out. This helps to restore the balance.
Linda:	I have tried to slow my breathing down but I forget to do so when I'm anxious.
Psychol:	The paper bag is an emergency measure which helps once you begin to feel all these sensations but you need to learn how to breathe correctly.
Linda:	And I seem to be tense all the time.
Psychol:	Yes, chronic muscle tension and over breathing often go together. Are you able to say exactly when you became aware of being so tense?
Linda:	I think that I have been anxious ever since I left Liverpool. That's my home town and the people are very friendly. I need people to be friendly because I'm quite shy, and I never make the first move.
Psychol:	Since we have some idea what is causing the anxiety, we can start to work on the shyness and loneliness and your feelings of insecurity.

PETER: aged 30, single and an engineer

| Peter: | Usually, I go to work by underground. A few months ago, coming back from work I suddenly began to feel faint and weak. I had to get out at the |

next station and sit on a wall for half an hour in the fresh air. Fortunately a bus came along and I caught that.

Psychol: What was going on in your life at the time this happened?

Peter: Nothing in particular that I can think of.

Psychol: What about earlier this year?

Peter: I split with my girlfriend. Well I say that – in fact she left me for someone else. That was a really bad time for me but I coped with it alright, I thought. I was very down.

Psychol: And has there been anyone since then?

Peter: There is a woman at work I'm very attracted to but I don't think that she's interested in me. I haven't got round to inviting her out. I don't think I'm ready for another girlfriend just yet.

Psychol: Do you think that anything in particular had made you feel worse on the day when you had those feelings on the underground?

Peter: It had been a difficult week for me. I had been asked to work late for two nights in a row. I suppose I feel it is always me who is asked to cover when someone is off sick. Sometimes it gets me down.

Psychol: You say 'Yes' when you mean 'No'.

Psychol: I always do... but that wouldn't make me feel faint and weak and panicky on the underground, would it?

Psychol: Perhaps feeling panicky and faint is a way of letting go of some of the anger and tension you build up. It makes you feel bad but it doesn't harm anyone else.

Peter: In my family, no one ever gets angry.

Psychol: I'm wondering how often you feel that you are being put upon or exploited and you don't react.

Peter: A lot of the time. In fact, looking back I let my girlfriend walk all over me. I didn't enjoy that but I thought that I would lose her if I objected or got angry... and I lost her anyway.

Psychol:	How have you been feeling since that first occasion when you felt so ill on the underground?
Peter:	I've got really bad. I've managed to get lifts to and from work, which is just as well because now I find that I can't manage the buses.
Psychol:	Is there anything else that you avoid doing?
Peter:	Shopping is a nightmare for me, particularly if I have to queue at the check-out. Once I had to write a cheque and the girl couldn't read my signature. I was so embarrassed when she called the manager. Oh and I can't use the launderette at all.
Psychol:	What about your social life?
Peter:	That was mostly at work. Now I'm terrified that I will stop being able to go to work. I love my job, and so far I have managed without taking much time off, but I wonder how much longer I shall be able to go on. I seem to be getting worse.
Psychol:	Are there other ways in which you feel you are getting worse?
Peter:	It's not just the feelings I get when I have to go out. Now I am waking up in the morning with a feeling that there is a tight iron band across my shoulders. I lie there thinking if only someone would come along with a pair of pliers and release me from the agony.

Treatment:

Peter recovered after a year's treatment using relaxation and a step-by-step approach to travelling and shopping. At the same time, we examined the way in which he thought and uncovered his extremely negative approach to life. This was how his parents had taught him to think. 'Take a pessimistic view and you will never be disappointed' was the family motto. More important, Peter had been taught to be extremely passive and unassertive. We role-played being more assertive and he enjoyed learning how to say what he thought and felt. He very quickly learned that being assertive is one of the best antidotes to anxiety.

Follow-up: 18 months after treatment began

Peter: I often think back to those days and am so thankful
            that I am better and that I can do everything now
            without those terrible panic attacks. Sometimes I
            catch myself wondering if they will come back. It
            is a comfort to know that if they were to come back
            I would be able to cope with them. I still do the
            relaxation every day and I make sure that my
            breathing is slow and even.

            Nowadays, most of the time, I manage to say
            what I want to say. If I don't manage it the first
            time, I think about it, and then I go back to the
            person and tell him that I didn't say what I wanted
            to say. I'm much more assertive now.

LAURA: aged 36, a single business woman

Laura: It all started by having 'the shakes' for no
            apparent reason, especially when I had to go out
            or anywhere far from home. I didn't realise
            straight away it was agoraphobia and put it down
            to overworking – I'm a bit of a workaholic you
            know.

Psychol: Can you think of anything else which might have
            triggered off these attacks or did they 'come out of
            the blue'?

Laura: There was nothing I could associate them with
            specifically. They just occurred out of the blue,
            even when I didn't feel particularly under stress
            at the time.

Psychol: Can you elaborate on that a little more?

Laura: Well, for instance, I might have a period of several
            good days and then have to face a very important
            Board Meeting at work and parry questions from
            the Financial Director whom I have crossed
            swords with in the past, and is no friend of mine. I
            managed this meeting very well and was proud of

myself. I was just beginning to think I had licked the problem and then, that evening, when I was doing the late-night shopping in the supermarket with my boyfriend whom I live with, I got a massive 'wobbly' over the frozen peas! [Laughing nervously]. It just doesn't make any sense, does it?

Psychol: Not on the surface, but sometimes agoraphobia can be the long-term outcome of other deeper problems which haven't been resolved, like bereavement for example. It is well known that an unresolved grief reaction can produce atypical results. Free-floating panic attacks and agoraphobia are sometimes evidence of this.

Laura: Well, it's strange you should say that because just over two years ago I lost my father and my maternal grandmother whom I adored but I wasn't able to cry at either funeral...I was too busy propping up my mother and the rest of the family and organising all the practical arrangements. Everybody said how marvellously I had coped at the time.

Psychol: And how long after that was it that you started getting these panic attacks?

Laura: Difficult to remember exactly, but I should say about a year. I remember the first attack was in the office at a meeting. I was drinking coffee and suddenly I felt my throat go dry and constricted and my stomach churned and I felt hot and sweaty and faint and my hands shook so violently that the cup started rattling. I was very embarrassed and had to rush out of the room and go to the loo and wait for it to pass. After that it would happen in the Tube on the way to work or when I was out shopping without warning. It all happened so quickly I was not able to nip it in the bud. I can't stand it, as I pride myself on being a super-efficient whizz-kid and a strong feminist who can tackle anybody and yet this has to happen! I don't want to depend on tranquillisers for the rest of my life so I hope you will be able to help get me off them.

As you can see from the above, agoraphobia can be non-specific, not solely the result of a panic attack associated with a particular situation or place but can 'come out of the blue' as a result of a long-term problem. In Laura's case, intensive bereavement therapy was necessary to help her with her unresolved grief before relaxation and anxiety management cured her problem.

JOHN: aged 42, married, runs a successful business

John: I didn't realise I was having panic attacks. I just felt hot and sweaty when I was in company and particularly in the pub. I felt I had to get out into the fresh air. Sometimes I felt faint and I wished I could faint. If I had fainted, I would have been carried out and that would have got me away.

Psychol: Do you think that there was something in particular about being with a group of people in a pub that made you want to get away?

John: Looking back now I can see that it was always the same fear: a fear of making a fool of myself; of not knowing what to say; of not being able to get into a conversation. I feared being asked questions to which I hadn't got an answer. Then there was the drink. I don't mind a few pints but there was always a great pressure from other people to drink and drink. In my business, everything seems to hinge on being able to drink pint for pint with clients and colleagues. A lot of drink just makes me feel ill.

Psychol: How did you cope with that?

John: After a while I avoided going to pubs or restaurants or football matches. If I went to a football match there was always the fear that I would be asked to go and socialise in the pub.

Gradually, I only began to feel safe at home. Even at home there was the threat of friends dropping in to see us and I would be forced to talk to them. My wife will tell you, I've never been one to talk much but we used to go out for a meal at least once a month and we enjoyed that. Then I couldn't face going out. I feel sorry for her. It's not much fun for her staying at home but I cannot stand the feeling of being trapped in a restaurant.

John was originally referred for treatment for his fear of going out. As can be seen from this fragment of conversation, his problems began when he became socially phobic and they gradually spread to a fear of going out and a fear of being trapped in social situations where he might feel foolish.

I have included this conversation to illustrate how one phobia may lead to another.

PAM: aged 35, works in publishing in London

Pam: My problem is that I just can't bear to use lifts or the underground any more. I have always travelled to my job by underground and used the lifts without thinking about it.

Psychol: Have you had an unpleasant experience in connection with the underground?

Pam: No. It happened after I got stuck in a lift in the supermarket. It was on a Saturday and there were several of us in the lift with our trolleys piled high with food and we were going down to the underground car park. Suddenly the lift stopped between floors. There was an emergency button and somebody pressed it but nothing seemed to happen. I was almost paralysed with fear. I remember one of the men in the lift saying: 'Well, we won't starve,' and I couldn't raise a smile. It felt like hours before we got out but in fact it

	wasn't very long. I was exhausted when I got home.
Psychol:	How have you been travelling to work since then?
Pam:	I've been taking taxis but it's costing me a fortune. I would do anything to get back my confidence in travelling. We're terribly busy at the moment so I really haven't got much time.
Psychol:	The quickest way to deal with your phobia is to flood yourself with anxiety and remain in the situation until the anxiety has gone down. If you can summon up the courage to go into the situation that you most fear and see it through, it is often not as frightening as you expected.
Pam:	I might be able to do that but not by myself.
Psychol:	At first, I will come with you and then you can practise alone. Before we begin, we need to be very specific about the particular aspects of the situation that frighten you.
Pam:	It's the thought of being under ground and unable to get out that really terrifies me.
Psychol:	Occasionally we use silver vaults for patients with claustrophobia because they are under ground. The vaults have steel doors and although the doors are open whilst the public are allowed in it feels rather like walking into a safe. If you feel motivated to face your worst fear, we can set aside a day and travel on the underground to visit the vaults.
Pam:	Would we need the whole day?
Psychol:	It will depend on how long it takes for your anxiety to come down. That is why we use the vaults. They have all the anxiety provoking qualities of a lift and you can stay there until you feel comfortable. If we leave before your anxiety has come down we shall just make the phobia worse. Since we cannot predict how long it will take, I think we should set aside a day but it is unlikely that we shall have to stay there all day.

The following week:
We spent Wednesday morning travelling on the underground to the vaults. Pam's anxiety was at its peak as we entered the underground and it was touch-and-go whether she would be able to get on a train. Pam was less concerned about going into the vaults. By the end of the morning she was feeling quite comfortable and told me that, as she couldn't afford to buy any more silver, she was beginning to feel bored.

Pam: After the first hour, it was really enjoyable looking at the silver and coming back on the underground I felt pleased to be able to behave like a normal person.

Psychol: Yes, you managed very well and now, ideally, you should practise on your own a few times. As you were quite comfortable in the vaults, it would be better to practise in the underground. Stay in the underground until your anxiety comes down and you feel comfortable.

Subsequently, Pam practised by herself just travelling around the underground system until her anxiety went down. Then, she practised the journey to and from her work and found that she had no difficulty.

At the follow-up a year later Pam was still able to travel easily and use lifts. The reason why the treatment worked so well was that there appeared to be no complicating factors in Pam's phobia and she was very well motivated.

EDNA: aged 75, disabled with arthritis and using a frame

Edna came to the clinic accompanied by her husband, Stan, very shortly after her problems began. She was fortunate in that her doctor referred her for treatment immediately and we were able to see her very quickly before the fears became entrenched.

Edna: It happened quite suddenly. One morning I found that I was terrified to go out by myself. The following day I was the same ... just terrified, and the next week it got worse. On Thursday, Stan and I went out as usual in the car. He left me in the car whilst he went into the post office. There must have been a long queue because he was gone some time and I became terribly fearful. My heart was pounding and when Stan got back I burst into tears and clung to him.

Psychol: And before that, you were able to go out by yourself with no difficulty?

Edna: Yes. I had been using my frame quite confidently for three years and I managed very well. My husband drives so we get out quite a bit.

Stan: I am so worried about her but I don't seem to be able to help. She doesn't like me to be out of her sight for a minute.

Psychol: Once your wife starts feeling afraid, she can't control the feelings?

Stan: That's right and she knows I'm worried about her and that makes her worse. She starts worrying about me.

Psychol: Can you give me a picture of your life together before all this happened?

Stan: Well I suppose we had been spending most of our time visiting sick relatives. Edna's brother and her two sisters have been ill for some time. Her brother is seriously ill with his heart and now my brother is ill. It has been one person after the other over the last year.

Psychol: How do you feel about all this visiting you are doing?

Edna: I feel very guilty if I miss a day. Stan gets fed up but he's very good about it. It has been a bit much and now Robert is ill it's made it even more of a strain.

Psychol: Do you think that you are also very worried that either you or your husband will become seriously ill?

Edna: I do worry about my heart although my doctor has

	checked on that, and of course I worry about Stan.
Stan:	It's also quite depressing doing the visiting. It's always the same conversations day after day. All they talk about are cancer and heart attacks.
Psychol:	It sounds as if both of you need a holiday. Would that be possible?
Edna:	It is possible. In fact a friend of mine did suggest that we come and spend a fortnight with her in the country but I couldn't. I would feel very guilty about leaving everyone.
Psychol:	Perhaps you would feel less guilty if I told you that it was part of the therapy. It seems to me that you have both been under a considerable strain for a long period of time and that all this visiting has become quite burdensome. Would you like to think about that for a week. Next week I will teach Edna a modified form of relaxation that she can do sitting in an armchair. The relaxation will help, but a fortnight's holiday might be much more effective.

Edna and Stan came back for another session the following week and told me that they had decided to go on holiday. They still felt rather guilty but they had realised that there was a connection between Edna's phobia and the roles they had been playing as sole caretakers for their families. Once they had made the decision, neighbours and friends had offered to visit their relatives during their absence. They could not arrange their holiday immediately so Edna spent three weeks just practising walking around the close where she lived going a little further each week and with Stan not far away.

After the holiday:

| Edna: | I lost all my fears when I was away and now I feel that I can get back to normal life, although I'm worried that the feelings will come back. |
| Psychol: | I think that the life that you were leading was not very normal. It was rather unbalanced. In fact it |

wasn't much fun. Now is the time to start looking after yourself as well as your relatives. If you are giving to them all the time, then there is nothing left for yourself. You need to conserve your energy and have some enjoyment. Perhaps you could cut down your visits to the sick.

Edna: I know that Stan would be pleased if I did. He feels quite resentful that we spend so much time with our relatives.

Psychol: It may be that you also feel quite resentful but you feel guilty about having such feelings.

Edna: I was brought up to believe that you should be un-selfish but I can see now that sometimes you do have to look after yourself. We had become very tired and gloomy.

I must stress that we do not have many patients who recover as quickly as this. It is quite possible, however, that such recoveries are common in general practice and that those individuals are not referred for psychological treatment.

FELICITY: aged 50, married with grown-up children

Felicity: I just seemed to slip into the habit of not going out. I'm not sure that I am agoraphobic.

Psychol: When did the habit begin?

Felicity: About a year ago.

Psychol: What was happening in your life at that time?

Felicity: Nothing in particular. It was just that I found that I couldn't bear being driven. I can't drive myself. My husband or my son have always driven the car and I went out with them a great deal.

Psychol: Had anything upset you when you were being driven?

Felicity: I've always felt slightly nervous of being driven, and last winter, my husband and I were on our way to Coventry and there was a multiple crash just ahead of us. We were not involved but I was very shaken. I occasionally go out in the car with my husband but I make him drive at about 20 miles an hour, and I won't let him overtake.

Psychol: The accident you witnessed was a year ago. I wonder what prompted you to seek treatment now.

Felicity: My husband is taking early retirement and we've bought a cottage in the heart of the country. With very little transport in that area, my fear is that I shall become completely housebound. We are moving in three weeks' time.

Psychol: Have you any other worries?

Felicity: No. I'm very happy about the move. My husband and I both paint and we are looking forward to having more time together to do the things that interest us.

Psychol: It seems that you have incubated your fear of being driven over the last year. There are two alternative forms of treatment. One is to practise very gradually in the situation and to tolerate a slight amount of anxiety each time. The other is to go into the situation you fear most and to stay in it until the anxiety comes down.

Felicity: I think it will have to be the quick method because we are moving, but I'm not sure my husband would be willing to do the driving. He thinks it's quite dangerous having me in the car.

Psychol: I will take you out in my own car and we will keep driving until your fear has subsided. You can sit in the back first of all and then you can move into the front passenger seat when the anxiety has come down. What would be the most frightening aspect of being driven for you?

Felicity: Going fast. Being in the outside lane. I suppose overtaking at high speed would be the worst.

Psychol: How high do you think your anxiety would be on a scale from 1 to 100?

Felicity: Close to 100.

Four days later:
We set off at 9 a.m. from the hospital and drove through the suburbs. Felicity started the journey half lying on the back seat with her eyes closed. She told me that she couldn't bear to see what was going on.

Psychol: I'm afraid this treatment won't work unless you are able to sit up and keep your eyes open and experience the fear. I will drive very slowly around the quieter streets until you feel able to sit up.

As we drove, I asked Felicity to rate her level of anxiety. As soon as her anxiety began to decrease and she could tolerate having her eyes open I moved on to busier roads. When she became comfortable with these conditions, she came and sat in the front passenger seat. Later on, I drove faster and took the car into the centre of town. At about 2 p.m. her anxiety was down and she was not at all anxious. At this point, I decided that we would join the motorway and we drove to the airport. During the journey I changed lanes from the inside to the middle and overtook another car on the outside lane at 70 mph. Felicity managed to tolerate all of this, although at times she had her eyes shut. We arrived back at the hospital at 6 p.m.

Psychol: How are you feeling?
Felicity: I feel perfectly all right. Just a bit tired.
Psychol: Do you feel like doing this again tomorrow and the next day?
Felicity: Yes. I can see that I am going to get bored rather than anxious.

PAUL: aged 19, a music student

Paul had fainted on a weekend concert tour and had been taken to a local hospital. This experience had left him feeling extremely anxious about his health and he had been unable to go out except with members of the family.

Paul: I worry all the time about collapsing when I'm out.

Psychol: When you fainted on tour that weekend were you given any explanation as to why?

Paul: Yes. I remember the doctor saying something about blood sugar and I thought I must have diabetes.

Psychol: In fact you were diagnosed as being hypo-glycaemic, which means that your blood sugar level had dropped below normal.

Paul: Mmn. I don't know why that happened.

Psychol: On that occasion there were at least two possible causes. You told me that you had not eaten for a large part of the day and you had also had an emotional shock. Either of those could have caused your blood sugar level to drop suddenly.

Paul: Mmn. I do try and eat properly now but I still worry about fainting. I hate the thought of people looking at me. It makes me embarrassed just thinking about it. And now I seem to be worrying about my heart.

Psychol: When you feel aroused in any way, you begin to overbreathe, then your heart starts to thump and it is difficult for you to think of reasons for these symptoms other than serious illness.

Paul: Yes. I can't think of any other explanation when I become anxious. I usually think the worst. On Saturday I got really worked up when I read in a newspaper that someone quite young had died of anxiety. My heart began thumping away and I got really scared. I started worrying about having a heart attack and not getting to a hospital on time.

Psychol: It was not difficult to see the connection between your thoughts and your symptoms on that occasion.

Paul: No! At the moment most of my thoughts seem to be anxious ones. I can't relax at all. I have tried doing the relaxation exercises but they just seem to make me more anxious.

Psychol: Are there any times at all when you feel more re-
            laxed?
Paul: When I am listening to music. I have several cas-
            settes that make me feel relaxed. I just sit and
            listen to them.
Psychol: It would be a good idea to use those cassettes to
            relax to and to set aside one or two periods during
            the day just to listen to them. Eventually, you may
            feel able to carry out the relaxation exercises to
            the accompaniment of music.
Paul: Yes. I'll do that. As a matter of fact I have always
            been a very edgy person so I'm not surprised that I
            have difficulty in relaxing. It's also why I look like
            a runner-bean.
Psychol: During the next week I'd like you to think about all
            the different situations that you have been
            avoiding over the past year and try to put them
            down on a piece of paper in order of difficulty. At
            the next session we will set up a 'target ladder',
            placing the least difficult situation on the bottom
            rung and then the nearest situation in order of
            difficulty on the next rung up and so on. We can
            start with a ladder that has ten rungs.

Next week:
Paul: I've written out the 'ladder' although I'm not sure
            about the exact order. Some of the things at the top
            I think I'm equally fearful about.
Psychol: Don't worry about that. Later on we may be able to
            sort out the order of difficulty. What we need to
            discuss is your ability to use your imagination to
            practise going into some of the situations that you
            avoid.
Paul: Oh, I'm useless at that. When you suggested
            thinking about lying in a peaceful place when I
            was trying to relax I just couldn't think of
            anything.
Psychol: Being able to practise in your imagination is

helpful to some people but it is not essential. We can start the programme in reality, and to do that I will ask you to fill in diary sheets so that we both know what you have been able to do. I will also ask you to rate the level of your anxiety on a scale from 0 to 10.

The next extract is taken from a session three months after therapy began. Paul had been filling in diary sheets giving details of the time he had spent away from home, where he had gone, and the level of his anxiety. Now that he was able to go out we were concentrating on the thoughts that appeared to maintain or increase his anxiety.

Psychol: From your diary sheet, Paul, I can see that you have been managing to go out quite often.

Paul: Yes. I've had a good week. I went out and bought some cassettes and I helped a friend set up his music centre. Mind you, I still like to have someone with me and I often get panicky.

Psychol: Have you been practising arguing with your panicky thoughts?

Paul: Oh yes. I got on a bus with Mike this morning. The worst time was waiting for the bus. I just wanted to go home or walk. Then when it came and I was sitting down I didn't feel quite so bad, although I found myself feeling my pulse all the time. My heart rate was a bit faster but I managed to tell myself that I had walked a long way before I got to the bus stop, and so that calmed me down a bit. Also, I suppose I had the thought: 'Goodness, I'm on a bus, therefore I should be anxious.'

Psychol: You managed to stay on the bus, which is the most important course to follow. If you manage to stay in the situation you learn to tolerate the anxiety and you learn that it does pass.

Paul: It did get better. Then I made myself anxious just at the end of the journey because I wasn't sure which stop to get off at and I wasn't sure that there was a stop just outside the hospital.

Four months later:.
The following is a short extract from a session after the Christmas holiday. Paul is now back at college.

Paul:	Yesterday I was in a group where losing self-control would have been really embarrassing and I was a bit twitchy but nothing to speak of.
Psychol:	Losing control would be what?
Paul:	Oh, passing out or having to rush out for some air.
Psychol:	What did you say to yourself?
Paul:	I tried to ignore the feeling and fortunately the group was interesting and fairly light-hearted. Then there was another meeting when I was quite tired and I thought that I was going to pass out. On that occasion I did argue with my thoughts. I said to myself: 'You didn't get much sleep last night, so no wonder you feel a bit dizzy and you can't concentrate so well.'
Psychol:	Were you able to believe your argument?
Paul:	Oh yes I was ... almost 80 per cent ... so I feel that I'm improving. The trouble now is that I want to make up for lost time. I had a terrible Christmas last year. Before Christmas, this year, I had a panic attack in a bookshop. My stomach was churning and I felt really shaky. I had lost a lot of sleep. I was so determined to enjoy Christmas that I worked myself up into a state. I got over-excited. I wasn't able to see that at the time but I worked it out afterwards.
Psychol:	During the Christmas holidays you seem to have dropped the little-by-little approach and been rushing up the ladder two steps at a time.
Paul:	Yes. I spent three-quarters of an hour on my own in the Shopping Centre and that was terrifying. It was so packed and I was frightened that people would look at me if I passed out. I felt light-headed. I get that feeling a lot.
Psychol:	Perhaps you are beginning to realise how often

your thoughts produce the symptoms of illness.

Paul: Yes. I have been practising arguing with the panicky thoughts. Sometimes, of course, I lose the argument. For example, I had agreed to go on a car rally on Sunday. I suppose it was the thought of being miles from anywhere and worrying about fainting or having a heart attack. I tried to think of all the pleasant things, such as the countryside we would be driving through, but I found I couldn't think about anything pleasant. I suppose I was wondering if there would be a hospital in the area. I began to feel quite ill.

Psychol: It looks as if you have been going ahead of your arousal level. For the moment, try to stay with the programme we have agreed and only depart from it if you feel very calm and confident that you can manage.

Paul: I'm scared that my symptoms will muck things up for me. On Saturday I'm taking my new girlfriend to the cinema and that means doing two things that are upsetting to me: as well as going to the cinema it means going on a bus. If only I could tell my girlfriend about my nerves she could be a great help because she might encourage me to do more things but I am frightened that I shall lose her.

Psychol: Clearly the relationship with your girlfriend has been the spur to all this activity and perhaps if she knew how you felt she could help you more effectively.

At the next session:

Paul: Last Saturday was the first time I went to the cinema alone with Lisa. Last time we went in a group. I tried to get my father to take us in the car but he had to go somewhere else. I even suggested taking a taxi but Lisa thought that was being really extravagant. In the end we went on the bus and I surprised myself by how calm I felt. At the cinema,

I managed to get us seats at the end of the row so that made me feel better knowing that I could get out easily if I began to feel faint. Afterwards I told Lisa about my difficulties. She seemed to take it all right. I was frightened she would think I was a wimp or a weirdo.

The following week:

Psychol: I noticed from your diary sheet that you have only made two very short journeys on the bus.

Paul: Yes, I thought you would have something to say about that. Really I'm quite a lazy person and since I've been ill I've been given quite a lot of lifts and I really enjoy going by car.

Psychol: I can understand your enjoying the small perks that you have had since these problems began. Some people become quite addicted to them and it makes it harder to overcome the phobic habits.

Paul: Well, much as I enjoy people waiting on me and going shopping for me, I would rather be able to be normal.

GERALDINE and PHILIP: aged 23 and 24 respectively

This young married couple arrived together for the first consultation. Philip works in the City and Geraldine is a beauty therapist. Geraldine explained that she couldn't bear being on her own. Her mother had died three years ago and this had left her feeling very insecure.

Geraldine: I have been thinking about my 'ladder of fear' and at the top would be staying in the flat alone all night. I don't think that I could bear to stay in the flat alone, even for a few minutes, when it's dark outside. That really scares me.

Psychol: It might be easier if we start the programme at the weekend when we can take advantage of the daylight hours. As a first step how would you feel if

Philip went out on Saturday morning and stayed out for, say, half an hour.

Geraldine: I think I could manage that so long as he doesn't let me down and stay out longer.

Psychol: To help your anxiety, plan to do something in the flat when Philip is out so that you are not waiting anxiously by the window for him to come back. If this step goes well then try the same step on Sunday morning.

One week later:

Geraldine: Well that was a disaster! On Saturday morning, as soon as Philip went out of the door, I put my fingers in my ears so as not to hear him going downstairs. When I did that I could hear my heart beating so fast I thought it would burst and that made me feel really panicky. I yelled out of the window and asked him to come back.

Philip: I didn't know what to do. I didn't know whether to go back or keep walking away. I was frightened something might happen to her so I went back.

Psychol: That seems to have been the right thing to do. Clearly that first step was too difficult for Geraldine to manage. Perhaps it could be made easier. Geraldine, would you feel safer if you knew that you could telephone a friend and talk to her whilst Philip was away?

Geraldine: I could ask Fiona to stay at home on Saturday morning. She's a close friend and she knows all about my nerves.

One week later:

Geraldine and Philip continued the programme together at the weekend. Fiona had agreed that Geraldine could telephone her if she needed reassurance when she was alone in the house. This offer had helped Geraldine to cope with the initial phase of the programme, which is often the most difficult part.

Geraldine: This Saturday, I didn't get the real burning panic
            feelings, just butterflies in the stomach. I switched
            on the radio as soon as Philip left so that I wouldn't
            hear his footsteps. I did the same thing on Sunday
            morning and then I spent most of the time on the
            phone to Fiona.

Later on that month the programme was accelerated because
Geraldine had 'flu and took sick leave. This meant that she
was in the house alone most of the week. Geraldine commented that towards the end of the week she hardly noticed
that Philip had gone.

Six weeks later:

Geraldine: I have made a lot of progress, but this week I have
            been feeling very depressed.
Psychol: Has anything happened that has upset you?
Geraldine: No...there doesn't seem to be any reason for
            feeling so depressed.
Psychol: Is this an important time of the year for you. Are
            there any anniversaries?
Geraldine: It would have been my mother's birthday last
            Saturday. [Geraldine became very distressed and
            tearful] I can't believe I still feel like this after
            three years.
Psychol: Maybe it is harder for you to deny that she is dead
            when her birthday comes round.
Geraldine: Yes. I think I felt like this last year. I know that I do
            think of her as still alive. The reason I put a hard
            mattress on the bed in the spare room was for my
            mother. She couldn't stand sleeping on a soft one.
            It's odd isn't it? She made me feel very secure.
            Whenever I felt ill or panicky she would reassure
            me and make me feel better.
Psychol: You have given me quite a rounded picture of your
            father but not of your mother. You always speak of
            her good qualities and how reassuring she was.
            You never talk about what you didn't like. There

must have been times during her long illness when
you got quite fed up with her.

Geraldine: I felt angry with her for leaving me ... and I did get
fed up with visiting that hospital.

Philip: And she still thinks that it was her fault that her
mother died.

Psychol: It must have been very painful for you that you feel
angry towards the person to whom you were so
attached.

Geraldine: Yes. It does make me feel guilty.

We worked for several months on Geraldine's ambivalent
feelings about her mother. I then suggested that we think about
terminating the therapy before the Easter holiday. Geraldine
agreed to do this but later felt angry with me. She commented
that, although she was able to be alone in the house, she
wondered if she was able to do this because she had the reassurance of coming to see me. Later on she commented that
leaving therapy was beginning to feel like another death. This
enabled us to bring to the surface some of the feelings,
thoughts and beliefs surrounding her mother's death and to
work on the process of mourning that had not been completed.
Once she was able to let her mother go, she found that she
could invest more in her marriage.

SANDRA: aged 24, and recently married to Ted. Sandra works as a florist

This is a series of conversations taken from several sessions
over a period of a year. There were many complex factors that
had led to the difficulties that Sandra was experiencing when
she came for treatment and which had contributed to her long-
standing problems of dependency and anxiety.

Sandra arrived with a very jaundiced view of professionals,
as she felt she had received very little real help. Her opening
remark as she walked into my room was: 'Well, this isn't going
to work.' Clearly she was depressed and angry about almost
every aspect of her life. I wondered out loud why she was
taking up this very fixed, angry stance.

Sandra: I have felt very unsafe for about a year. I think that the first time that I had a real panic attack was on the bus going to work.

Psychol: Was there anything going on in your life that may have made you feel insecure?

Sandra: We had just moved to London and I had started a new job.

Psychol: Have you been able to travel on buses since then?

Sandra: Not on my own. I can go to work in the West End if I go with a friend but if the bus gets caught in traffic then I panic. I feel clammy and my stomach churns and I feel that I am going to faint. My husband comes and picks me up from work in the evening.

Psychol: What other situations do you have difficulty with?

Sandra: I can't go on buses in strange places even when I'm with someone, and travelling on the underground or in aeroplanes is completely impossible.

Psychol: What do you feel comfortable doing alone?

Sandra: Shopping. At least, I don't mind going to the local shops and I can go to the shops near to where I work.

Psychol: Are you aware of any other problems?

Sandra: Well, I feel tense all the time and I seem to cry a lot ... and I'm really quite irritable. One of the girls at the shop said, 'It's a good thing you're having therapy as it may improve your temper.' I don't think it's a good thing. I've tried taking tablets and that helps a bit but I don't really see how you can help. What's talking going to do for me?

Psychol: I understand your feeling of hopelessness and that seems to be related to your depression. The irritability may also be part of the depression. The therapy programme I am going to suggest is quite an active one but we shall go slowly until you are feeling better.

Sandra: I'm on anti-depressants but I don't want to be on them for ever.

Psychol: Now is not the time to stop taking them just as you are about to tackle your fears, and in any case you would need to stop taking them gradually. Your doctor will advise you about when and how to cut down. I will keep in touch with her and let her know how you are progressing. Meanwhile, perhaps we should look at some of the other areas of your life. You were married very recently and you moved to a new flat in London. I wonder how you feel about those changes in your life?

Sandra: I often feel very down and irritable in the flat. It's very noisy. I can't get away from the noise from other flats. I feel very cooped up in there and we don't go out very often.

Psychol: It is not hard to see the changes in your life that have contributed to your depression and your fears. Would you describe yourself as a person who has always felt rather anxious and insecure?

Sandra: Oh yes. I hated going to school as a child and I would think up excuses so that I could stay at home. I remember my mother taking me to the doctor when I was 9 because I kept having tummy aches. He said there was nothing wrong with me. I'm quite a nervy person, but at one time I could travel by myself.

Psychol: When you have these panic attacks, what do you think is happening to you at the time?

Sandra: I keep thinking that I am going to become ill, although I am in quite good health. My husband tells me not to worry but I can't help worrying.

Psychol: It would be helpful if you could give me a picture of your life.

Sandra: Mostly, I work. I haven't got any hobbies except knitting and I can't go anywhere because I can't travel very far.

Psychol: It seems that your life has become very restricted since your marriage.

Sandra: Yes. It's not a lot of fun.

Psychol: Would your husband be able to help you if we

	designed a therapy programme to start you off travelling on buses alone?
Sandra:	He could help with coming home in the evening, I think.
Psychol:	As you are very tense I will teach you how to relax and then ask you to imagine you are travelling on a bus. In that way, being relaxed will become linked with travelling on buses. At the moment, high anxiety and tension are associated with being on a bus. We want to change that association to feeling calm and relaxed while travelling on a bus.
Sandra:	That sounds as if it's going to take forever. Can't you get me better any quicker?
Psychol:	There is another method called flooding. That means going into the situation you fear most and tolerating the anxiety until it goes down.
Sandra:	Oh NO! I'd die if I had to do that. I must say I don't feel very hopeful about this therapy. When do you think I will be able to go on a bus alone?
Psychol:	After you have visualised yourself travelling on a bus alone. When you feel ready, you can start the programme in reality. It will be very gradual. Initially, it will be just a matter of travelling to one bus stop, then two and so on until you feel comfortable travelling as far as you want to go.
Sandra:	I don't think Ted really understands all of this. He thinks that I am mentally ill. Sometimes I wonder if I'm becoming schizophrenic.
Psychol:	No. You are not mentally ill and I think that it would be helpful if Ted came with you to these sessions and we could talk about your problems and worries together.
Sandra:	I think he'll come, but he'll be a bit embarrassed. He's not one for talking. I usually do it for him... and he's even worse at listening!

As you can tell from this extract, Sandra was depressed, irritable and extremely tense, but not too depressed to start a therapy programme to manage her anxiety. She was highly motivated to learn how to relax and to control her breathing. She found it easy to imagine herself in a peaceful place and used this to deepen the relaxation. As soon as she was able to achieve a state of deep relaxation, she started to practise, in imagination, getting on a bus and travelling one or two stops whilst visualising as far as possible all the aspects of the route she was travelling along and the scene inside the bus. She was advised that, if she started to feel tense, she should stop her imaginary journey and go through the relaxation procedure again until she felt completely relaxed.

Six weeks later:
Ted has joined Sandra for the third time.

Sandra: I was just thinking coming here this morning that I won't be able to go on one of those driver-operated buses.

Ted: Yes, you will. One bus is the same as any other.

Sandra: No it's not. I know I would feel trapped on one of those buses. Sometimes I wonder if Ted understands my problems.

Ted: No, I don't understand but at least I do try to understand. I'm here, aren't I?

Psychol: It's not often possible to understand completely what these problems are about. We can still manage to treat them using the approach that I have described and perhaps as time goes on we shall be much clearer about the underlying causes. We can use our weekly sessions to talk about how Sandra is feeling and the relationship between your thoughts and your feelings.

Sandra: I'm getting quite good at the relaxation. At first when I tried thinking about getting on a bus I got really tense but now I can calm myself down.

Psychol: As soon as you feel the tension do you go back in your mind to your favourite spot, relax for a few minutes and then try again?

Sandra: Yes. I always think about a place in my friend's garden under a weeping willow. I just lie there in the grass and imagine the branches moving above me in the breeze. It makes me feel very calm and peaceful.

Psychol: Good. It's very helpful if you can use the same picture each time because it will become a cue to deep relaxation. Try and imagine the branches of the tree moving in time to your breathing.

Sandra: Sometimes I get so relaxed I fall asleep.

Psychol: If it's not convenient to fall asleep, set an alarm clock or a cooking timer to wake you up.

Sandra practised taking imaginary journeys. Her practice sessions took 30 minutes and she did them twice a day.

Two weeks later:

Sandra and Ted
Sandra: I'm feeling much more confident now and a bit more cheerful.

Psychol: Good. The next stage of the programme is for you to start travelling on a bus alone for one stop only. Would it be possible for you, Ted, to arrange to wait in your car near a bus stop close to where Sandra works? If you do that for a week without any problems then next week we can plan the second step.

Ted: Well, I'm quite willing to do that but why can't she try and do the whole journey at once?

Psychol: That is an approach that some people choose and it is called flooding. In the first session, I discussed with Sandra the different ways of tackling her problems and she preferred the step-by-step approach. Our aim is to increase the distance travelled very gradually and for Sandra to learn to tolerate a small amount of anxiety. In this way she should avoid any further panic attacks.

Sandra: It will be very strange for me not having anyone to talk to on the bus.

Psychol: When you are on the bus, try to distract yourself from dwelling on the strange feelings. Perhaps you could plan the meals for the next few days or think about where you want to go for a holiday next year. Before you get on the bus, decide what you are going to think about. If you forget what you intended to do, just look around you and count the number of times you see a certain colour.

Sandra: I'll try to do that but what should I do if I get anxious?

Psychol: Attend to your breathing. Try to slow your breathing down and make it regular. Then continue to talk to yourself reassuringly. We can spend the last 20 minutes of this session practising some positive self-talk.

Sandra: Ted is probably better at that, he thinks all this is easy.

Ted: No, I don't. It's just that you get so worked up about things.

Psychol: Positive self-talk is not about telling yourself that something is easy when you don't think it is. Talking positively to yourself is a way of reminding yourself of what you already know. You forget the coping techniques very quickly when you become anxious. You know that if you attend to your breathing and relax your muscles you begin to feel much calmer. If you tell yourself that you are beginning to feel ill, you will start the process that leads to panic. For example, saying: 'If I attend to my breathing, my muscles will relax and I shall feel calm,' is a much more positive statement than: 'Oh, here I am, on a bus on my own, I know I'm going to feel ill.'

Sandra: People on the bus will really think I'm mad if I start doing that.

Psychol: They will if you say it out loud. The positive self-

talk we are practising is to replace what is already
going on in your head. It is to replace your long-
playing, anxiety-provoking record which you find
very alarming but are used to.

Ted: I think that I am going to try a bit of that when I'm
driving. I do talk out loud and it's unprintable.

Psychol: No doubt, you are both feeling the strain of dealing
with these problems. It would relieve the tension
for both of you if you could spend at least one
evening out of the flat. You have mentioned that
you both like sports and you have a very well-
equipped sports centre near to where you live.
Doing something active is another very effective
way of becoming relaxed.

Sixteen weeks later:

Ted and Sandra have joined a sports club and are enjoying
playing tennis and swimming two evenings a week. The bus
programme is going well and there is now only one more bus
stop to achieve on the route home. There have been some setbacks, including difficulties when Ted's car was out of action.
Fortunately, we had made an alternative plan in case this
happened. We had agreed that Ted would travel on the same
bus but out of Sandra's sight. He stayed on the top of the bus
and Sandra sat downstairs.

Sandra: As you can see from my diary there were one or
two occasions when I felt too anxious to continue
the programme and that made me feel rather depressed. Still, I feel that I have done well and I
haven't had any panic attacks.

Psychol: Will you feel able to travel home by yourself on the
bus next week?

Sandra: Yes. I feel I can cope now because I know what to
do when I get anxious.

Three weeks later:

(Sandra had missed two sessions)

Sandra: Well, I've had a very strange few weeks. I did the journey home by myself for the rest of the week that I saw you and it went very well. Then the following Monday, I felt terrible on the bus going to work and I had all the symptoms that I had at the beginning. I felt sick and faint and I was sure that I was going to have a panic attack.

Ted: I had to take her in the car the following day. I thought: 'Well, that didn't last very long.'

Sandra: I was determined not to be beaten and so I got Fiona to come with me on Wednesday, but I still felt panicky and ill. I didn't go into work for the next two days. Then, at the weekend I realised that it might be something else. I went to my doctor the following week and discovered I was pregnant.

Psychol: As soon as you felt sick and faint on the bus, you sent your brain a message saying: 'This must be a panic attack,' rather than, 'I might be pregnant.'

Sandra: Yes. I'm over the moon about being pregnant and I'm also very pleased that I haven't gone back to the bottom rung of the ladder.

Psychol: Congratulations on both. Thinking that every sensation is the start of a panic attack is something that happens to many people who are highly sensitive to such changes. They pick up the smallest cue and attribute it to something that they fear. I'm very glad it turned out to be such good news.

Ted: I did say that I would rather she had had a panic attack but I really didn't mean it!

In August of the following year I received a card from Sandra and Ted posted in France and telling me that the flight was lovely. The fact that Sandra was able to fly to France suggests that, once the basic principles of the therapy have been learned and applied, further improvement can be expected long after the formal therapy finishes. When Sandra completed her treatment, she didn't even want to consider travelling by air and was quite content with what she had achieved. Obviously her general sense of security had increased and this was partly owing to the fact that the marital relationship had improved considerably.

Index